The Idea

The
Idea

the SEVEN ELEMENTS
of a VIABLE STORY
for SCREEN, STAGE,
or FICTION

Overfall Press

Erik Bork

Overfall Press
4607 Lakeview Canyon Rd 379, Thousand Oaks, CA 91361
www.overfallpress.com

Printed in the United States of America

Cover Design by Domini Dragoone
Cover photo © StillFix/123rf
Author photo by Lisa Gerber

ISBN 978-1-7327530-1-3
e-book ISBN 978-1-7327530-0-6

Library of Congress Control Number: 2018956851

For every writer

who for the first or thousandth time

has tried to come up with

a great story

Table of Contents

Acknowledgments

This book is a product of three decades of studying and working at screenwriting as my primary vocation, including the better part of a decade teaching the craft at institutions like UCLA Extension and National University and as a mentor to hundreds of writers of various levels, around the world. In working with them, I began to codify a body of knowledge, opinion, and advice that led to the principles outlined in this book. And so I'm indebted first and foremost to all of those writers who came to me for guidance and feedback and trusted me with their work. Colleagues in my teaching and writing careers have also helped me tremendously, especially Tom Hanks, who gave me my start as a professional writer and employed me on project after project, with all the charm, intelligence, passion, and easygoing generosity you would expect from him. The amazing producer Tony To helped me make good on those opportunities on the miniseries *Band of Brothers* and *From the Earth to the Moon*, the projects for which I am still best known. I also have to thank Brett Loncar, my longtime television packaging agent at CAA, who was a key figure in helping me to understand what makes a viable premise in TV—mostly by shooting down so many that weren't, but also by advocating passionately for those that were. Finally my wife, Margaret, an immensely talented singer, songwriter, and creator of musicals, has supported me and been my biggest cheerleader as I develop my own projects and help others to do the same.

INTRODUCTION

It seems like things should be getting easier for writers.

There are more resources than ever to finish a book, a web series, or even an independent film and put it in front of people. In this age of self-publishing, digital video, and social media, almost any of us can create and share our work without having to impress powerful gatekeepers.

But if we want to reach a large audience beyond personal contacts and online followers—and actually make money with it—that's another story. Getting lots of people to pay to watch or read what we write—and turning it into a profession—is still elusive for almost everyone.

Things really haven't changed much since the old days, when we needed agents, publishers, producers, and big companies behind our work for it to ever have a chance at reaching a mass audience. Even today, the overwhelming majority of successful movies, TV series, books, and plays still go through these traditional systems.

And unfortunately, it's no easier to impress those "gate-keepers" than it ever was. That's the sad truth we writers grapple with whenever we finish something and send it out into the world. We usually don't get back the love that we were hoping for.

Why not? What are those people looking for? Why is it so hard???

The answer is actually pretty simple. These elusive conduits to a potential audience and career respond to the same things audiences do: a great idea that's well executed—one that grabs them emotionally, holds their attention, and powerfully entertains them.

But most of the time, they don't get that. It's not even close, in their minds. They're severely underwhelmed by more than 99 percent of what they receive. So they move on to the next submission—as quickly as possible. And the writer is sent either a bland rejection or no response at all.

As a result of this frustrating process—and the difficulty of getting true engagement from anyone who could move one's work forward—we often assume the real problem is that the doors are too closed and the decision makers too hard to reach. If only we could get our work into the right hands! Then we'd have a shot!

But what I've learned in my years as a professional screenwriter—and in mentoring others who want to become one—is that "reaching the right people" is really not the hard part of succeeding as a writer.

The hard part is creating something that the "right people" would be excited by if they read it.

And that's what most of us never quite achieve.

Why not? Where is the disconnect between the excited writer who thinks they're onto something and the "industry" that disagrees? What turns these tastemakers off and makes them stop reading or decide to pass?

Part of it is an obvious lack of professional-level execution in the writing, which seasoned readers can pick up on pretty quickly. And just a few pages of that convinces them that the rest of the work probably isn't worth their time. Because it almost never gets better from there.

But believe it or not, that's not the main issue most of the time. What usually sinks a project, instead, lies in the basic idea for the story—what we might communicate in a "logline" of a sentence or two, or a brief synopsis in a query letter, or a quick verbal pitch.

Most of the time, it all ends right there. The reader is not intrigued enough by the idea. They don't see potential. They don't need to read the whole piece to make their decision. They know that the core idea is the most essential, foundational element in making a project viable in the marketplace. And most ideas they see (and scripts or manuscripts they read) lack a central idea that they think really works.

This "idea" is the core premise or concept of the story, which basically comes down to the answers to the following five questions:

1. Whose story is it, and why should we identify with them?

2. What do they want, in their life circumstances and relationships?

3. What's in the way of them achieving that?

4. What are they doing to try to resolve this? What makes it so hard?

5. Why does it matter deeply—to them, and hopefully, to us?

This is a story's basic DNA. And a reader's interest in a piece of material (or lack thereof) tends to stem directly from the answers to these questions.

How I Arrived at This

It took me a while to figure this out.

When I moved to Los Angeles from Ohio after college to try to become a professional screenwriter—and started working as an office assistant at 20th Century Fox studios—the screenplays I was writing, in my free time, did not meet the criteria laid out in this book. Nor was I even aware of these criteria. I was merely trying to emulate what I thought were the key elements of movies I loved—without understanding them on a deeper level. I obsessed about story structure and scene writing (like most writers), but I didn't really know how ideas worked. I didn't realize this was something I needed to study, nor did I know how to study it.

That's because most books on screenwriting—then and now—don't spend a lot of time on just the idea. There is so much to say about story structure, character, and the writing process itself (not to mention navigating "the business") that picking what to write in the first place often gets short shrift. And writers often give it short shrift, too.

I had a vague understanding that the biggest Hollywood screenplay sales were mostly "high-concept" ideas, but these were usually in action or fantasy genres that didn't strongly appeal to me. So I wrote my "low-concept" comedy/dramas inspired by real life. They might have been decently executed. But they went nowhere.

Then I switched gears completely and took a course in sitcom writing at UCLA Extension. After that, I set out to write "spec" scripts for existing shows such as *Frasier*, *Mad About You*, and *Friends*. With those, the need for a great and bold original idea didn't apply as much. I only needed a "small" idea for an episode of a series that someone else had come up with, and then to execute it really well. Doing this eventually got me my first agent, and it ultimately made my boss in my day job take notice of my writing.

Fortunately, that boss was Tom Hanks (I'd been assigned to his production company from the Fox "temp" pool that I'd been floating around in for two years), and he had a project for me to help with—which became the HBO miniseries *From the Earth to the Moon*. His generosity in giving me a chance to ultimately help write and produce that project changed my life. A few years later, I got to play a similar role on *Band of Brothers*, another miniseries that he executive produced for HBO—this time partnered with Steven Spielberg.

Both these projects were historical limited series adapted directly from nonfiction books. So they were a different animal from what most writers are trying to do—which is come up with an original idea for a feature film, novel, play, or TV series. I didn't have to do any of those things—I just had to learn how to adapt these true stories about real people and events into compelling television. (Not that that was easy, or that I didn't make a lot of mistakes and go through a steep learning curve.)

Thankfully, both of these projects were successful and got my foot in the door of Hollywood as a writer. They led to the opportunity to pitch my own original ideas for drama series to the networks. This meant I was back to having to come up with my own, brand-new, fictional ideas. I didn't have the crutch of an established series or nonfiction book to lean on. It was all on me to come up with "the idea."

So I began coming up with premises for drama series. And I soon learned that it was a lot harder than it looked. My own agents rejected most of my ideas as not worth pursuing before I could even get close to pitching them to potential buyers. I realized there was a lot I didn't understand and needed to learn.

This is when I started seriously exploring "what makes a successful idea" for TV. As I made this my full-time job (in the one-hour drama marketplace), I eventually started arriving at some ideas that my agents liked, and which I sold as pitches to networks—meaning, they hired me to write pilot scripts for them.

Later, when I began teaching screenwriting and mentoring aspiring writers, I noticed that they were almost always starting from an idea that lacked some of the key ingredients that I'd learned were essential. But they didn't know it. And unfortunately, none of the hard work they did to execute these ideas could ever overcome those core issues.

This happens to virtually every writer, on most projects. Including those written by professionals.

So I began codifying what the key elements of a commercially viable film or TV series idea seemed to be, based on my experience—so I could teach them to others. (This also helped me in my own writing, as you might imagine.) I blogged about these and shared them with writers I worked with. And I began to see that they also applied to fiction, theater, and other forms of "story" beyond screenwriting. And that's what led to this book.

It might not be easy to arrive at a really winning idea, but it's also not brain surgery. There are simple and clear elements that are generally present in the best ideas. One can study them and work with them. It just requires getting out of the mind-set that "it's all about the finished script or manuscript." It's not. Yes, the writing has to be executed at a very high level. That's a given. But even more crucial than execution—than the words on the page of the final product—is the basic idea behind that product. Everything hinges on that. It really is an "idea business."

In this book, I will present what I've come to believe are the seven elements of a successful idea for a story. They can be distilled down to a single word each—which we'll get to in the next chapter.

But before we do, three quick caveats:

1. My goal is to help writers looking to sell their work and make a career of it. Artier or experimental films, plays, or works of literary fiction might fall outside this purview and still receive acclaim on a niche level. I'm focusing on ideas with potential American mass audience appeal—this means commercial fiction and theater and the kind of film and television that is widely distributed. In other words, the kinds of stories writers might be paid to write and lots of people might pay to consume.

2. I am primarily a screenwriter. Though I believe the ideas in this book apply equally to other media for story, for the purposes of simplicity, I will use words like "script" and "audience" where one might substitute "book/manuscript" or "readers," for

instance. When I do use the term "readers," I'm usually referring to the professional readers a writer needs to impress to move their work forward (including agents, managers, producers, publishers, and paid readers who screen material for them).

3. A television pilot is a very different animal from a screenplay, novel, or play, because rather than telling one single story with a definite ending, it is meant to introduce a series—which is a container for a potentially endless number of smaller stories, usually for a variety of different characters. So each chapter ends with a section on how to specifically apply the book's principles to the unique medium of television.

1
FOCUS ON THE IDEA

When a writer finishes a script, they generally understand that it's time to get feedback on it, preferably from objective professionals—or others who are knowledgeable and serious about the craft—who will give them their unvarnished opinion, hard as that might be to hear.

What they usually don't do is seek out the same sort of feedback on their idea for a story before they spend months or years writing it. But that's the point at which they have the most leverage over what the finished product will look like. That's when they're making the most important creative decisions about it that they will ever make.

Why don't they? Maybe they're worried about their idea getting stolen. Beginning writers often obsess over this, whereas professionals rarely give it a second thought. While it's true that one can't copyright a one- or two-sentence idea for a story (as opposed to its specific expression in a longer document like an outline or script), it's also true that ideas are rarely stolen, and even if they were, they would usually lead to very different scripts from the one the original writer would have written.

But I think the bigger reason is that for most writers, idea generation and evaluation is a painful and amorphous process, and it seems like nothing is really happening—until they're writing scenes, or at least structuring a story. Playing with story ideas doesn't feel like "writing." But it is—and it's the most crucial part of the process.

Agents and managers who represent professional (or near-professional) writers understand this and insist that their clients run their ideas past them before they commit to writing. They will shoot down most of them, and typically have lots of notes on the ones they don't, because they know they can't sell something if it's not based on a really strong idea. And they don't want their clients wasting time writing a script that is flawed from the get-go.

As a screenwriter, I have ignored this fact at my own peril. And as a mentor to other writers, I have seen how universal this problem is. Of the hundreds of scripts I've read from writers who haven't worked professionally yet, virtually all of them had a central idea that was significantly flawed in terms of the principles I lay out in this book. Meaning that if I had heard the idea before they started writing it, I would've tried to convince them to rethink it in a significant way. Ninety percent of my most important "notes" or criticisms on a script are concerns I would have voiced about the basic idea if they'd run it past me before writing it.

So the number one piece of advice I now give to writers is this: get serious objective feedback on the idea *before* you launch into structuring or outlining—let alone writing the script. And expect people to have notes on the idea, and for you to have to do some substantial rethinking, before you ever get past that stage. This can go on for a long time and involve lots of different ideas that you get temporarily excited about. Most of these will never quite take or win over professional readers. This means that the finished script probably wouldn't, either. Wouldn't you rather fix that now, instead of months down the road? So whatever you would do to get high-quality feedback—whether it's from writer friends or a paid consultant—do that with the idea.

The 60/30/10 Rule

I would say that 60 percent or more of what makes a project potentially successful (or not) is the core idea that could be communicated in a short synopsis of a few sentences up to a single page. And this is all that industry professionals will generally be willing to look at to consider whether they want to read further.

Think of it: 60 percent of what's most important to our chances is what is contained in that mini-pitch of our basic idea. It's mostly not about all those months of outlining, writing, rewriting, and getting feedback—that's not the most important part. The most important part is what comes *before* all that.

But the work in coming up with that basic idea is not easy. It can take a lot of time and much trial and error to arrive at one that could garner the interest of professionals. Most of us don't want to spend that much time questioning our core story premise. But the reality is that "the business" will question it, and will usually dismiss it—and all our hard work—unless we have an idea they see as viable.

Many if not most writers never come up with a story idea that solidly addresses the criteria in this book, despite years of pursuing the craft. And this is a big part of the reason most never end up selling anything or becoming professionally employed. They might focus on bringing their scene writing and narrative structure up to professional quality, but not on their understanding of what makes a viable idea. Which is arguably the most important thing.

If there's nothing else you take from this book, please take this "60 percent" figure and reconfigure your efforts toward "basic idea" development accordingly. Spend more time and energy on ideas. Make it your number one goal as a writer to learn what makes a great one and to get better at generating them.

Once you have an idea that really works, and you feel reasonably sure (because you've vetted it thoroughly with others), then, and only then, does it make sense to turn to the other 40 percent of the process.

What does that consist of?

To me, 30 percent of what's important in a project's success lies in the structural choices, the decisions about what will happen, scene by scene, in a story—or what you'd see in an outline.

That means only 10 percent is about the actual words on the page—the description and dialogue that people will read in the finished product. The actual scene writing—that's the last 10 percent.

This seems shocking to many beginning writers. Ninety percent of what matters is what's *behind* those written pages—what the writer worked on before they ever fired up any script-formatting software.

Again, I'm not saying the writing doesn't have to be really top-notch for a script to advance a writer's career and move forward in some way. Of course it's best if your scene writing is memorably great, and your structure and outlining choices are very strong, too. I'm just saying those two things are not the key factors that determine a project's success. And in fact, those two things usually are never even considered or seen, because the project's chances die at the earlier idea stage.

And when they die, it's for one simple reason: the idea struck whoever read it as insufficient in one or more of the seven elements that this book will focus on—elements that are universally understood as key, even if different readers would use different terminology to describe them (or might not even be conscious of the fact that these are what they look for and respond best to).

So without further ado, here's what they are . . .

The PROBLEM

At the heart of any story is a problem that takes the whole story to solve. It's a challenge that the story's main character is actively engaged with, which consumes their attention, energy, and emotion—and that of the audience. It usually starts by about 10 percent into the story and continues until essentially the very end (having built and become worse and more difficult along the way), when it's finally solved.

An idea for a story really *is* that central problem. It's about what the main character is faced with and/or trying to achieve—its difficulty, its importance, what's in their way, and what they do to try to resolve it.

These are the things that professionals want to understand from any logline and/or synopsis. Until they can see the problem in this way, and until they think it sounds really viable and intriguing, they won't want to read anything else.

So what makes a "problem" (i.e., your basic story idea) viable?

It needs to have the following seven essential characteristics, the first letters of which form the acronym PROBLEM:

1. **Punishing.**

   Not only does it take the whole story to solve the problem, but the main character spends virtually every scene trying to solve it. But they can't, because it is so vexing and complicated—and it generally only gets more so as they try to address it. If it didn't, it wouldn't take a whole "story" to overcome. The problem defies resolution and besieges the main character as they grapple with it.

2. **Relatable.**

The main character of a story—and what they're dealing with and why it matters—is easy to identify with on a human level. Because of this, we in the audience are able to strongly care that they reach their desired outcome, making us want to stay with the story. We even put ourselves in their shoes, such that it feels like their problem is our problem. We stay invested because they do. They remain active, and they keep trying to address whatever it is, despite all the slings and arrows that come at them in the process. If they didn't, it would feel like things weren't moving forward in a compelling way, and our interest would slacken.

3. **Original.**

Something about the premise of the story and its approach is fresh and brand-new—even though it also fits within the conventions of good storytelling and genre. There is a spark of uniqueness to the idea, and preferably to the writer's voice, as well.

4. **Believable.**

It's easy for someone hearing or reading the basic idea to understand and buy into it, even if it requires taking a leap and suspending disbelief, in some clearly defined way. In other words, it all feels real. The characters seem driven by identifiable human wants, needs, and behavior. It all sounds like it adds up, makes sense, and doesn't leave people asking any "why" questions or being skeptical or confused about anything.

5. **Life-Altering.**

The "mission" to rise to the central story challenge is of huge importance to characters the audience has come to care about. If it doesn't get solved, life will be unthinkably worse for them. Something in their outer life circumstances, on a primal level, is at stake. And if they solve their problem, things will be so much better than they are. All will be right with the world. In addition, the process of going through this challenge may alter them internally, in a hugely important way. But it's the external stakes that come first.

6. **Entertaining.**

   The process of trying to solve the story problem is fun to watch or read, consistent with its genre. Whether it's comedy, action, suspense, etc., the material creates desired emotional experiences in the audience, of the kind that they came to the project hoping to have. So it becomes like candy to them—something they want more and more of, something they really enjoy and would spend time and money on.

7. **Meaningful.**

   The audience comes away feeling that value has been added to their life—that something worthwhile has been explored, which has resonance beyond the time they spent watching/reading it. It was really *about* something more than just its surface plot—something meaningful to them.

Sounds simple, and even obvious, right? Fulfill these seven characteristics with your idea, and you'll have a piece of material that could get you the interest of a manager, agent, editor, or producer.

Or maybe it doesn't sound so simple. Maybe it sounds impossible to do all these things at once. If you're a little overwhelmed by the task, then you're probably recognizing what a big job it really is.

There's a reason such a tiny percentage of aspiring writers succeed, and why those who do are so handsomely rewarded. It's rare to successfully achieve all of this in a script or in an idea for one.

When we look at our favorite stories, they probably do it so effortlessly that we didn't even notice. These criteria are so basic to our experience of consuming good stories, that they might seem to be self-evident. But that doesn't mean they're easy to pull off. The reality is that it takes a lot of work to create what might appear effortless. And writers don't usually instinctively get what it takes to achieve this.

How "High" Is Your Concept?

In Hollywood, the logline is the standard tool for expressing the idea behind a movie or series. It is typically no more than a sentence or two, and it distills the premise down to the basic problem being faced. A good logline suggests a story that would clearly meet the criteria set out in this book. It presents a compelling situation for a character or characters that one can imagine audiences caring about.

And it lays out a central challenge that sounds really difficult, and entertaining to watch, such as:

> *A slick German industrialist profiting from World War II becomes sickened when he sees what's happening to the Jews, so he starts employing them, to try to keep them out of the clutches of a psychopathic Nazi camp commandant he's become friendly with. (Schindler's List)*

> *A naive recent college graduate gets involved in a secret affair with a married friend of his parents, whose daughter they think he should date. (The Graduate)*

> *A down-on-her-luck maid of honor seems to be losing her best friend to a richer, prettier, more confident married woman, so she sets out to defeat her and prove that she's the better bridesmaid. (Bridesmaids)*

When we talk about an idea for a story, we're really talking about something that could be easily understood in this short form—which is generally true of the most sellable ideas.

Successful loglines often have a "high-concept" element. "High concept" means an outrageous situation of some kind, not necessarily fantastical, but extreme, unexpected, unlikely, and with obvious entertainment value and broad appeal. Usually they come from a "what if" question, like "What if there was a theme park with dinosaurs that got loose?" or "What if a teenager time travels to the past and gets in the way of his teenage parents' meeting, so he has to get them together, then find a way back to the future?"

But even some non-fantastical premises can be called "high concept" if they are intriguing and clear and make the potential audience start conjuring entertaining images in their minds right away. "What if a forty-year-old man was still a virgin, and his sex-obsessed male coworkers tried to fix that?" Consider the original poster for this movie. Just the image of Steve Carell and the title alone is almost enough to make one get the comedy and challenges in this premise. It seems pregnant with possibility and makes one wonder why nobody ever thought of it before.

In a compelling logline with a high concept element, it's clear what the idea is, and why it's compelling. There's enough there that one can really picture the story. No one needs to ask a bunch of questions to understand what it is. They instantly "get it."

Nailing the Logline

Loglines can be a struggle for writers. Not because it's so hard to write up a sentence or two that contains these key elements, but because their story itself doesn't really contain them.

Ideas that lack some or all of the seven PROBLEM elements will usually reveal that fact in their loglines. As such, loglines are a useful tool for professionals when deciding whether to pass on reading a script. And that's the logline's main reason for existing—and for buyers to want to see only a logline before committing to read further. Because 99 percent of the time, they can tell from the logline that they don't want to read further.

So the challenge isn't in writing the logline. It's in coming up with an idea for a story that is so viable as a PROBLEM that it will be easy to describe in a logline. Then it's a relatively simple matter to express its essence in a sentence or two.

Having said that, there are some guidelines to follow in crafting one. Our goal is for the reader to be able to picture the movie (or series, stage play, or novel). It shouldn't "tease" the story while leaving out key information. It should clearly communicate what the main story challenge is and why it's difficult and important.

A film producer or executive looking at a logline wants to be able to imagine the poster, the trailer, the audience, and the genre. They want to be able to see how this idea clearly fits within a certain type of movie that tends to work with audiences—and how it's a unique and engaging variation on that.

So a good logline generally includes three basic elements:

1. A quick sense of who the main character is, which makes them seem relatable in some way.

2. The "catalyst" that launches the story—meaning the event that changes everything and leads the main character to have to act.

3. The nature of the challenge they now must face, their mission in solving it, and its huge difficulty and importance.

That's really it.

Two quick examples:

(1) A man raised as a joyful, innocent elf at the North Pole (2) learns he's human, and heads off to (3) find his father and his place in the world,

in a city where his childlike goodness seems to be rejected: New York. (Elf)

When (2) a mafia boss is shot and incapacitated, (1) his youngest son—a war hero who was never supposed to be part of the family business—decides he must (3) take over to try to defeat the rival mob families who are gunning for them. (The Godfather)

The key thing that's often missing is number 3. That's the most important part to get across. The most commercially viable ideas have a "mission" of some sort for the main character, which will take the whole story to accomplish, be incredibly difficult, and in all likelihood go badly for much of it—even if the mission is simply to try to escape a bad situation. The audience is meant to become emotionally invested in this character and mission, and be entertained by watching it.

There might also be an "inner journey" the character goes on—an arc of growth and change. But that is not what we're trying to communicate initially—it's secondary. The logline usually doesn't focus on this, or on what the character has to learn. Instead, it lays out what they want and what's in the way—in terms of both outer life circumstances and relationships with others. It ideally makes people think, "What an enormously difficult and fun-to-watch challenge!"

2

PUNISHING

Audiences are basically sadists.

We like to watch people go through the most hellishly life-altering ordeals, and the worse it gets for them, the more engaged we are, as long as there is some hope of success, which the characters are actively pursuing. Whether it's a horror film or a comedy or a true story like *Hamilton*, we tune in to watch people be punished, and we enjoy seeing characters pushed to their absolute limits and beyond. We seem to like our main characters frustrated, beaten down, devastated, and humiliated, and yet passionately, almost insanely driven to try to reach their goals.

Why? I think on some basic level, we consume stories because they are inspirational examples of people trying to rise above. The problems characters face in stories tend to be exaggerated beyond those in our normal lives—which is part of what makes them entertaining. But on a deeper emotional level, we can still relate to and get caught up in the characters' attempts to better their situations, and we become invested in the possibility of them defeating long odds to come out on top. And when they do so, we feel like *we* have done it with them.

But the success can only come at the very end, if at all. There might be glimmers of positive forward motion in the middle, but only glimmers—and these generally have to be immediately followed by things getting worse (or at least a reminder that things, overall, are still pretty bad). This is true from the first emergence of the main story problem all the way to the final climactic battle in what screenwriters call the third act of a movie. The focus is on the difficulties: difficulties that worsen, complicate, and defy solving.

The legendary Broadway writer/producer/performer George M. Cohan is supposed to have once said: "In the first act, you get your main character up a tree. In the second act, you throw rocks at them. In the third act, you get them down." The nature of what that tree is, and what those rocks are, is key. You could even say that "story = main character + tree + rocks."

And that's the main thing any agent, producer, or executive is looking for in a logline, synopsis, or script: "Why should I emotionally invest in this character and what they're grappling with? How is the tree big and important enough to make me feel something? How might there be enough rocks to escalate the story all the way to the climax?"

Ultimately, we want the audience to care deeply while being fascinated and entertained by what is happening. This caring only tends to occur when they're watching relatable people struggle and improvise in the face of some sort of hellish siege—where they're undertaking a huge challenge that they're sure to lose but which is desperately important to all being right with their world. This is true whether they're facing life-and-death stakes or seemingly smaller everyday matters, like you might see in a comedy.

In 2013, an anonymous professional script reader working for the major studios created an infographic that explored the common issues with three hundred screenplays they had been paid to read (of which only eight were deemed worthy of a "recommend"). Most of these scripts were probably submitted by agents, meaning they came from writers who had already conquered the first major hurdle that most aspiring writers never achieve: getting professional representation. Still, many of the most commonly observed problems relate to things not being "punishing" enough.

Take these three criticisms from the top ten in terms of how frequently they showed up in scripts this reader had evaluated:

1. **"The story begins too late in the script."**

   In other words, there isn't a big enough problem and active effort to solve it until much later than there should be. I often see scripts where the third act has a major challenge as the climax, but prior to that, there isn't anything big, difficult, and punishing enough that the main character is actively besieged with and trying to solve.

2. **"The scenes are void of meaningful conflict."**

   On a scene level, there isn't enough difficulty and conflict that advance and evolve the status of the primary story problem. This is something scenes should typically do. If this isn't happening, there's likely a larger problem with the concept, because the best stories provide endless scenes of difficulty that mainly only get worse until the very end.

3. **"The conflict is inconsequential, flash-in-the-pan."**

This is another way of noting that the problem isn't big and enduring enough throughout the script, and/or the stakes of solving it are too low.

So even in professionally submitted scripts, the top two most common issues are lack of "conflict" or problems (otherwise known as "story"). Often, there's not a big enough overall problem to rest a whole movie on.

"Not being punishing enough" is the most common overall weakness I've seen in the hundreds of scripts that I've read. It's more common than not that the main character doesn't have a big enough overall problem, or a high enough level of difficulty as they try to solve it. Things are just not "problematic" enough in terms of what they're facing.

If you look closely, even characters in the lightest of comedies are probably in some version of hell and struggling to get out of it. No matter what good things might happen along the way, they have some overarching problem that seems to be in the way of their ongoing happiness, which is the focus of the narrative.

Degree of Difficulty

Successful stories tend to center on one big problem that emerges early on and is not resolved until very close to the end. The main character is directing all their efforts toward trying to solve it. They're not just sitting around, living life. They're actively engaged. And it's what we, the audience, are there to watch them do: engage.

If this main character is actively trying to solve their problem and reach their goal in virtually every scene, what does that tell you about the nature of that problem, which defies solving until the very end?

It's difficult.

So many stories get tripped up because the problem just isn't *hard* enough to sustain the entire story. There isn't enough build, enough evolution, enough changing of the game. The main character isn't impacting the situation with their actions, causing it to change, but then also facing the consequences of that, in terms of increased conflict and ongoing complications.

At the heart of a viable story idea is a problem that develops in this way—one that's thorny and defies resolution. The challenge of solving it gets more problematic and yet more important as the story plays out.

A good logline for an original story idea would instantly communicate how this is going to be the case: how the main character faces a seemingly impossible challenge, which could go wrong in a million different ways (and probably will) before it's resolved.

> *An accident cripples the Apollo 13 spacecraft on its way to the moon, and mission control must find a way to get the astronauts back to Earth alive, with extremely limited resources and options. (Apollo 13)*

> *Three groomsmen who lost their about-to-be-wed buddy during a night of drunken misadventures in Las Vegas—which they have no memory of—must try to retrace their steps in order to find him in time for the wedding. (The Hangover)*

These two examples are polar opposites in terms of genre, but both suggest how difficult the challenges will be right away, and anyone who has seen these films can remember how punished the characters were as they tried to pursue their goals.

Even in a comedy, the difficulty of what the main character is trying to do still seems huge to them and beyond their abilities. They are ill-suited to the task at hand, and the deck is completely stacked against them. What they're trying to achieve seems extremely unlikely—but we can imagine it will be fun to watch them try.

The same is true in successful TV series. The characters are under siege virtually all the time, in one way or another. What they're trying to accomplish is beyond them. But they keep pursuing it. The difference is that movie (and book and stage) characters generally reach that goal at the end of the story (unless it's a tragedy), whereas TV characters will only resolve some short-term crisis but won't ever really get what they most would like to have—whether it's ownership of a successful company in *Silicon Valley* or control over their mythical lands in *Game of Thrones*. Every episode will find new ways to deny them that. (More on this later, in the chapter's TV section.)

So, when we're looking for an idea for a story (or series), what we're really looking for are problems, more than any other single thing—problems that will defy our characters' attempts to solve them.

I personally struggled with this for years. My first attempts at screenwriting were met with the criticism that my scripts needed "more conflict." I thought conflict meant people fighting, and my favorite movies weren't filled with fights and arguments. But eventually I realized that "conflict" really means people who want something they can't have, who are dealing with major life challenges and hard-to-reach goals. Yes, this typically leads to inter-personal issues, where characters are trying to get others to do what they want, but it doesn't always look like two adversaries at cross-purposes trying to defeat each other.

What it does always look like is difficulty. And in the strongest stories, the difficulties are constant. They're ever-growing and ever-evolving. The moment they stop growing (or even seem resolved) the tension comes to a stop, as does the audience's reason to care.

In my view, earning audience investment is the number one goal and challenge for every writer. "Why should I care?" is the note that I most fear on anything I write—because it's our most important objective and the hardest to achieve. Readers who "don't care" usually won't say that to our faces (thank God), but unfortunately, that's what they are most often feeling. And it makes them give up on a piece of writing.

Isn't that how we all are? We want to care, and if we don't, we tune out.

So, what makes us care? It's seeing someone we feel a connection with battling a big problem and becoming emotionally invested in a certain outcome for them, so much so that it's almost like it's happening to us—and the problem looks nearly impossible to solve.

Great Stories Are Like Great Games

Over the years, I've been a fan of various sports teams, and I like watching big games where everything is on the line for my team. At one point, something clicked for me as I realized that this sort of entertainment experience is very similar to watching or reading a great story—in any medium.

Certain elements need to be present for a sporting event to be the most engaging, to keep me glued to the TV screen: high stakes, intriguing backstory, relatable emotion, an awesome opponent, lots of ups and downs, and, finally, a come-from-behind victory. It's a difficult battle for the team I'm rooting for, all the way through, and it looks like they will lose, right up until the very end.

Doesn't this describe a great movie, book, play, or TV episode just as much as it does a big game?

I first had this insight while reading several scripts in a row: it seemed too easy for the heroes to win, or they seemed to be succeeding a lot in the second act and were clearly more powerful than their opposition.

In thinking about why these were not engaging to read, I found myself remembering games where my favorite NBA team (the Lakers, of course) was winning by twenty points throughout, and the other team never made it close.

Because of this, I could barely be bothered to keep watching.

As I thought this through, I came up with a list of seven specific qualities we tend to look for in a "great game," which I think apply equally well to "great stories":

1. **The difficulties of this game are huge—they're facing formidable opponents and seem overmatched.**

   The best main characters are not favored to win and really have no business thinking they're going to be able to. It's much more exciting to see someone rise to the occasion and be David fighting Goliath than to follow someone who seems to be the strongest, most capable one in the story as they go out and kick butt. Even superheroes need powerful super villains who are beating them, and who look likely to win right up until the final battle of the story. In every viable genre, the forces that oppose the main character's goal seem to have the upper hand throughout. (In other words, the struggle is "punishing.")

2. **The players have an engaging story involving adversity of some kind and positive qualities that make us connect with them.**

    This is why coverage of the Olympics includes filmed clips of the athletes in their home environment prior to the competition—to help us care about them as people. Reality shows often do the same. A great game is always better when there is some relatable, emotional human element that gives what's happening more meaning to us. In a good story, we need the same thing—strong reasons to connect with the main character, even before the competition begins.

3. **The stakes of this game couldn't be higher—it's a once-in-a-lifetime opportunity that will change the team's legacy or the players' lives forever.**

    Professional readers always look at the "stakes." Is there something big enough at risk here that demands audience engagement? Think of great stories like this: they usually chronicle the single most important turning point in a character's life, which will forever change them. Their life will typically be much better if they solve the story problem, and much worse if they don't. It really matters. They have something huge and relatable on the line.

4. **Far from running away with the game, or building a big lead early and holding it, the "home team" finds themselves facing unforeseen difficulties and complications.**

   A star player gets injured. The other team is prepared for what our team brings and counters effectively. Turnovers, errors, and great plays by the opposition (antagonists) give them all the momentum. In the best games (stories), our team (main character) is losing for most of it. And things gets worse and worse, until it seems like they have no chance of winning.

5. **The team plays with passion and persistence—picking themselves up from numerous crises—and continues in pursuit of their goal.**

   They may doubt themselves at times, but they continue to strive to meet each challenge. They make do with what they have, adjust on the fly, and despite all the problems, they stay in the game and keep trying. Our team/main character continues to try to solve their problem, even though most of what they do doesn't work and leads to complications that only add to their difficulties.

6. **Nevertheless, they find themselves significantly behind as things draw to a close.**

   Near the end, things may even seem hopeless and lost. Their efforts have come up short. But some new idea, new hope, and new plan emerges. However, even this isn't easy to pull off. They don't just come back and trounce the opponent. They claw and scrape and get knocked down, and the tension builds to one final climactic moment. It's the bottom of the ninth, with the bases loaded and two outs . . .

7. **Our team comes from behind, with one last push.**

   Finally, they are able to dig deep and find another level of play that they didn't know they had. They find their best selves in some way. Miraculously, against all odds, they rise up in the final moment and take the game—in the most dramatic fashion. This victory resolves all the tension in a satisfying way, inspiring a feeling that it will have a lasting impact for our beloved team. (Or sometimes, they lose, and it's more of a tragic feeling.)

So, let's recap. The best games to watch are *punishing* for the viewer's team, who they *relate* to personally. It's *original* in that it's never happened before, even if it's similar in some ways to past games. Of course it's *believable*, because it's really happening. The stakes seem *life-altering*, and it's exceptionally *entertaining* to watch. And for the biggest fan, it might even seem *meaningful* on a deeper level.

These qualities apply to sports (and viewers who love them) across cultures. And they also apply to stories. They seem to be universal elements that we, as audiences, need in order to be most compelled and engaged in the "contest." Sometimes they occur naturally in a sporting event. (When they don't, it tends to be a boring one.) We writers have to bring them to our stories. They don't just show up on their own. They require our creative action.

Adapting True Stories

If we look at events that happen in real life, they rarely play out like this. They don't have the structure of a "story" the way we're defining it. They might have some of the PROBLEM criteria, but they usually require a writer to sort through, edit, manipulate, exaggerate, add to, and fictionalize in order for the relative chaos of "history" to take on the patina of "story."

And yet true stories are constantly looked at as possible source material. And they might seem to writers like they will be easier to pull off, because the facts give them something to cling to, and to hide behind. There's not as much creative work to do. At least it appears that way.

I created a class at UCLA Extension called Finding the "Story" in True Stories for screenwriters. In it, students don't focus on writing a script. They don't even start the script, or even a scene-by-scene outline, in our ten weeks together. Instead, we focus on looking for whether there is truly a viable movie story contained within the piece of history that they want to write about—and how to turn it into one, in terms of concept and basic structure.

Usually I find that there isn't enough there, initially, in terms of a clear main character with a singular important problem that gets worse and worse as they try to address it, and which they only resolve through a "final battle" at the end. "Real life" typically doesn't give us that. So that's where the work begins.

Often students will show up with stories about the first person to achieve some particular worthy or impressive thing. And I generally approach these with two main questions. The first has to do with stakes: Why is it so important that they achieve it? What will happen if they don't? Will today's audiences desperately care that they reach their goal? If so, why? (More on this in the Life-Altering chapter.)

The second question is: How hard is the process of trying to reach their goal? Generally speaking, the big achievement that students want to write a movie about will only be compelling to an audience if reaching that goal is an absolutely hellish battle, if it looks like the main character will never win, and if, despite endless effort, the goal just seems more and more unobtainable. It's not so much the big achievement itself that makes it a movie, it's the punishingly difficult process of getting there—combined with the high stakes the audience can identify with and feel something about.

Apollo 13 (on which I proudly have the credit "Assistant to Mr. Hanks") is a great example of a true story that seems to contain all the required PROBLEM elements. Things just get worse and worse and more and more complicated, and the sense of importance, difficulty, and high stakes just grows and grows as the damaged spacecraft tries to get back to Earth.

Argo seems to be another good example, with its stirring "final battle" of getting the embassy workers through the Tehran airport and on a plane to safety without being found out by the Iranians. But guess what? In truth, there was no real "battle" to get through the airport. Their plan went off without a hitch. They walked right through to their plane without incident. No one questioned them. They didn't have to explain their supposed roles on a film crew. Their tickets didn't get canceled and need reinstatement. And nobody chased after the plane.

But what kind of an ending to a movie would that be? Instead of showing things as they happened, the filmmakers decided to depict what the greatest fears were of the people involved (and the audience), milking the suspense and difficulty of their final escape, beyond what really occurred. The basic arc of the story is historically true, including their eventual escape and their cover stories. The movie just makes it all harder than it really was, at least in this final sequence. We can argue whether that makes it less viable as history, but it's hard to argue that it doesn't make for a stronger movie.

That's the kind of thing professional writers typically have to do with true stories—the same as they do with fictional ones. And it's usually not just about upping the climax. Often, when one really analyzes the historical source material for a potential movie, it's hard to find the "one big problem" that takes the whole story to solve, because real lives are not about one problem. They're about a disparate mix of situations that don't evolve in the focused way that stories do. Writers usually need to find or create the "story"—a carefully structured dramatic sequence of events—rather than just try to show everything that happened and expect that to work.

But even when we find that one clear, finite problem/goal to focus on, the actual events often don't help us in making sure that the main character is continually, actively in pursuit of their goal and encountering complications that only build the difficulty. Real life just doesn't work that way, most of the time.

If it were a fictional story, it might be obvious that one needs to provide that rising action to the audience. But in a true-story adaptation, writers tend to think that because the events are real and an important part of history, some of their job is already done and the audience will be inherently interested, and forgiving, if things meander a bit or don't build that much or aren't singularly focused on one problem that the main character is actively battling.

I don't think that's usually the case. The audience does not make exceptions for true-story adaptations. And I learned this the hard way, by writing scripts professionally for a number of historical projects. What I gleaned from those experiences was that it's our job as writers not to transcribe history, but to find our "take" on it. To find the story within it that we want to tell, and then to tell that story, using (or creating) what serves it and not using what doesn't. Hopefully, it's true in spirit and even in many of its details to the history we're writing about. But it's still "ours." Only we could have written it the way we did.

To tell any story, "true" or not, requires a lot of creating. For one thing, we're making up virtually every line of dialogue spoken, because the history books (and even what the real-life subjects might tell us when they recount their story) don't give us their exact dialogue. They also don't give us the details of actions and confrontations that a screenwriter would need when writing scenes.

All of this forces the writer to make their own choices, which usually means detaching somewhat from the facts of the story—and from any people feeding the writer those facts.

I first learned this approach from writer-producer Graham Yost (*Speed, Justified*), in his approach to writing episodes of *From the Earth to the Moon* and *Band of Brothers*, which we worked on together. He would first familiarize himself with the history of what he was tasked to write, then he would put the research away and decide on the story he wanted to tell. Then he would write that story, without slavishly going back and forth to the research throughout the process. When he had a draft he liked as a story, he could then go back and vet it against the research to see how far he had strayed from the truth.

Usually the answer was not as far as he might have thought, and not in ways that needed drastic alteration to be close enough to the truth of what happened. And what he had was a strong story as a foundation for future tweaking.

I highly recommend that approach, as opposed to the more typical one, that I used to use, where the writer obsesses over the historical source material and goes back and forth from what they're writing to the research, hoping for it to supply the whole story, nervous about making up anything.

Whether a story idea is based on or inspired by facts or is completely made up, the process is largely the same: first and foremost, we look to challenge our main characters to their core, with something that will demand resolution, but defy all attempts to get it—right up until the end.

Television and the "Web of Conflict"

There are a few fundamental differences between how story works on television and how it works in the singular, closed-ended stories we find in books, movies, and plays (and even "limited series" or miniseries):

1. In television, the problems go on and on—so whatever the central thing is that plagues a character, it can't fully be resolved, or the series would end. As a result, their lives aren't significantly "altered" at the end of a half hour or hour, either externally or internally.

2. A series is not just "a story." It's a delivery system for potentially endless smaller, episode-long stories. Each installment needs to have a beginning, middle, and end, in terms of specific problems that are unique to that episode. These need to resolve in

some way, so that each hour or half hour stands on its own as a complete story experience, even though the larger issues that drive the series remain unresolved.

3. Television is much more of an ensemble medium. Most series have multiple "stories" in each episode, each with a different "main character" dealing with a different problem and goal they're focused on that week. This means that multiple characters in a series have to be relatable enough—in terms of who they are and what they're facing—for the audience to care enough to want to follow them. (Most movies, by contrast, have a single main character, and the audience sees everything through their perspective.)

With a series, we're looking for a big, overall, problematic situation that affects all the characters and that will never quite be fully resolved—until, perhaps, the final episode of the final season.

The challenge in TV is not so much about identifying a single main character with a single problem and giving them some sort of character arc. Instead, it's about finding a group of interconnected people who will have constant problems and conflicts the audience relates to, which can achieve limited and partial resolutions—but not to the point where their lives dramatically change and their main problem ends.

As with film, determining the nature of the punishment—of the "hell" that characters will be in—is key to the premise of any series. TV characters are generally "punished" by their relationships with other characters—and in the personal interactions involved in trying to solve their problems and reach their goals.

Modern Family cocreator and co-showrunner Steve Levitan once laid out a technique he used for developing series ideas by focusing on the characters. He was talking about comedy especially, but I think his process works just as well for dramas.

He recommended that we take any two characters on our potential show and think through their basic life situations. Who are they? What is their personality, the nature of their problems, and their place in the world?

He used the example of *Cheers*, with the washed-up ex-athlete who runs a bar and is charming but shallow—a ladies' man with no real meaning to his life. The show's creators then added an overeducated, elitist young woman who kind of looks down on such people but who just got dumped by her snooty fiancé and is stuck waitressing there.

Each character is very specific and easy to imagine, and it sounds like their interactions with others could be entertaining to watch.

Then comes the key thing. Levitan said to draw a line between those two characters. That line represents the dynamic between them. And that line is, essentially, the show. In other words, the conflicts inherent in that relationship (and other key character relationships) is the main story engine for the series and the heart of the concept. (Unless it's a "procedural" show about solving murders and the like—although even those usually operate on this character level, as well.)

So, we look for what happens when two specific characters interact. What's fun about watching it? How does it have the potential to lead to problems, for one or both people? How does it poke at their basic issues, and some big hole in their psyche, and their life?

Doing this takes some work. And probably some brainstorming. But Levitan's advice is to not stop until you have something really solid—something that "crackles." We're looking for a dynamic we would want to watch—one that's relatable and emotional, for both parties. We're looking to be kind of excited about the pairing of those two people, and the scenes and stories that could be derived from that.

Once we're solid with that, we then choose another pair of characters and do the same thing. When we're finished, every single character should have a vibrant dynamic with every other character. Added together, these dynamics feel like a "show." They have the potential for endless strong comedy and/or high drama.

And that's what they did with *Modern Family*, arguably the most successful comedy series of its time.

Think about how much devotion that took! That show started with ten series regulars. Granted, some of them don't interact with certain others all that often, but the creators took the time to come up with an entertaining and intriguing dynamic that each could have with each of the others.

There's a patriarch and his much younger, beautiful wife. She has a son. And that son has a very specific and entertaining relationship with both his mother and his stepfather. And if you put that son, Manny, together with his pretty (and older) step-niece, you had another fun dynamic: Manny has an unrequited crush on her. And if you put the patriarch together with his son-in-law Phil, you have something else: a man trying to impress a guy who will never respect him. Put Phil with the patriarch's young wife, and you have nervous lust. Put that wife with Phil's wife, and you have a prickly competitive conflict, where the daughter can't accept her father's new wife, who wants nothing more than this family to love her. Et cetera, et cetera.

At the end of the day, this entertaining web of conflict is the foundation of virtually every high-quality series idea. Developing it to a place that feels really solid before writing a word of a pilot (or even pitching the idea to anyone) is, to my mind, time and energy well spent.

"Punishing" Checklist

If your idea can live up to this five-point mission state-
ment, it should be "punishing" enough:

1. It's about one big problem that takes the whole
   story to solve. (In TV, it can essentially never be
   solved.)

2. What my main character(s) want(s) seems
   extremely unlikely and difficult to achieve, but not
   entirely impossible.

3. The difficulty of the problem will push my main
   character(s) to their limits as they actively,
   continuously try to resolve it.

4. These actions will lead to consequences,
   complications, and conflicts they didn't expect,
   which require further action.

5. The problem will grow through the middle of the
   story (or episode) until all seems lost. Only a huge
   final battle will resolve it.

3

RELATABLE

We want our main character to be punished. But we also want to tell the story in such a way that the audience feels personally identified with this character so that they really care about what happens.

We're basically trying to get strangers to feel strongly about someone they've never met. Ideally, these strangers make that person's problems as important to them—for two hours—as if they were their own. Saying it this way emphasizes how hard this is to do. It doesn't just happen naturally.

There are two aspects to achieving this:

(1) Making the character someone the audience can relate to, sympathize with, be fascinated and entertained

by, and/or want to see succeed. Part of this is about who the character is, and part of it is about what they're facing. The more they get beaten up by other people and events (especially when it's undeserved), the easier it is to feel for them.

(2) Telling the story from that character's point of view so that the audience can fully understand and share their perspective, their emotions, what they're trying to do, and why it matters to them.

Many scripts don't do one or both of these things. And because of these "main character issues" or "point of view issues," it's hard to really connect with the story.

The Role of the "Main Character"

"Relatable" is really a mild word for what the best stories achieve: they make the audience become one with the main character and experience everything as if it were happening to them. Across genres in successful stories, whether it's *Pretty Woman*, *Jaws*, or *Hamlet*, the audience feels what the main character feels and can't help but start to want what they want. This is what it is to be "emotionally invested" in the story, i.e., "really engaged and wanting to see what happens." This, of course, is every writer's goal.

Achieving emotional investment starts with understanding that any story really does have only one main character—the one whose perspective the audience is focused on and learning and experiencing things through. (But you might find multiple stories, and thus multiple main characters, within some movies, books, or plays, and almost all series.) The main character is the audience's point of view on the story, and the one they most relate to, understand, and, usually, root for.

That means that the main character is typically in nearly every scene of their story, and other characters don't get many moments separate from them—aside from a brief "cutting to the bad guy" scene in a movie like *Die Hard*. The story is essentially the main character's experience of it—it's all about their problems and goals and what they're doing in the face of those. Nothing else really matters.

Main characters are generally not mysterious. What they are trying to learn about others might be, but what's driving them at every moment needs to be apparent—what they think and what they feel. When these things aren't clear, the audience tends to lose that emotional connection. If they don't know what the character they're following is engaged in at any given moment, or why, they tend to become confused and detached.

The best main characters are also not passive. They're actively engaged in something that's hugely important to them. They keep going, despite lots of difficulties. If they give up, or just let things happen to them without taking meaningful action that affects the situation, then they become harder to care about and root for, and less fun to watch. It stops being their story. Audiences invest in the struggle and improvisation in pursuit of an objective, not in characters who are only "acted upon." And if it's a big enough problem to be worth telling as a story, the main character doesn't rest until it's resolved.

Other characters are affected, interested, and involved, but we see them through the main character's eyes, in terms of how they affect what the main character wants and is trying to do. We look *at* them, but *through* the main character.

If a story is told "objectively," where the reader is looking "at" all the characters, and not focused on what one particular person is wanting, feeling, and trying to achieve, the reader feels on the outside of the story and less engaged. This is one of the main reasons they will stop reading and pass on the project.

Subjective Point of View

The first script I wrote professionally was an episode of the HBO miniseries *From the Earth to the Moon*. I had been given an amazing opportunity by Tom Hanks and HBO.

And I was totally out of my depth. I had been writing spec sitcom episodes and didn't have any idea how to approach this kind of dramatic true-story adaptation.

But I knew enough about "story" to pick an episode that seemed like it was about one clear main character with a problem. Some of the episodes seemed to have this potential much more than others.

The one I chose was about the first American in space, Alan Shepard, and his fall from space-flight glory when an inner ear disorder grounded him. This forced him to work behind the scenes as a kind of "boss" to the other astronauts, but unable to fly himself and unhappy about it. Eventually, though, he found a cure, in time to be put back on active flight status, command the Apollo 14 mission, and land on the moon.

Sounds like a clear "story," right?

It did, but when I embarked on writing the first drafts of the script, I got so caught up in the research—and the responsibility of accurately documenting all the key events of the mission this episode was focused on—that when I gave the script to a more experienced professional writer involved in the project, he clearly didn't care about the story. He was nice enough not to put it that way. What he said was that he thought it needed a clearer point of view.

He didn't just mean that this character needed to be at the center of events—he already was. What was missing was that the audience needed to experience what he thought, felt, and wanted more from inside his perspective, and *everything* I depicted had to be about that—not the dry facts about what caused problems for him and his mission, which, not being life-threatening, were mainly of interest only to space junkies.

This episode (like all successful stories) had to become an emotional journey for millions of people, which starts with making it one for the main character and staying focused on that. It was not enough for audiences to be somewhat interested in his situation and the mission he ended up flying on. The real goal was for them to *care*—to relate to this human being and strongly want him to achieve the goal this story was focused on.

After many more drafts, I pushed the script as far as I could in the direction of a subjective emotional experience for Alan Shepard, and tried in every scene to focus on how his "one big problem" and goal was evolving—making sure that it kept evolving, with him actively grappling with it at the center of every scene. Eventually, the script was accepted as good, and I was asked to do some additional writing on other episodes. Which, let me tell you, was a huge relief.

The Relatable Center

A good idea for a story has a situation at the heart of it that virtually everyone can relate to, because it explores some fundamental human desire and/or problematic situation.

Blake Snyder's *Save the Cat!* screenwriting books offer ten "genres" that can really help writers to identify the best such situation for their idea—and to make sure that it has one. His theory is that successful movies seemed to be about one of ten different kinds of human problems, and he gave them fun names like "Dude with a Problem" and "Fool Triumphant."

I love using these story types while developing an idea, whether it's my own or brought to me by another writer I'm working with. Each one centers on a different type of hugely challenging situation that we can all relate to, and taps into something primal that we all share as human beings. Audience members either have been in such a situation or can easily imagine how difficult it would be—and may have had dreams or nightmares about something similar.

Stories are not about intellectually interesting things (although that might be a side element). They are about emotionally impactful things. There's a key difference. Our goal is to get the audience to *feel* something, not just to think something. And audiences pay to consume stories because they want that. They want to be led on an emotional journey, where they really relate to the central character and their predicament.

Sometimes writers get caught up in the intellectually interesting (to them) details of a science fiction world they've created, for instance, or the experiences of a military unit in battle, or a miscellany of real-life events in a true story they're adapting. But the audience doesn't usually want to be sifting through such facts and details. The core of a story needs to be easy for the audience not only to hold in their hands and understand but to feel something about. It should wear its heart on its sleeve. Most successful projects are about fundamental, universal, emotional things like good vs. evil, urgent threats that must be stopped, and once-in-a-lifetime challenges that will forever define who a character is and the life they get to live.

The Eight Types of Story Problems

Usually the relatable main character of a successful story is dealing with one of the following eight types of problems:

1. Someone or something is trying to kill me (or us).

2. Someone or something is trying to destroy my life as I know it.

3. I have a once-in-a-lifetime but incredibly difficult opportunity to rise up and be somebody, in a big way, that could forever change my sense of self.

4. I have to rescue someone from a potentially terrible fate.

5. I have to reach a distant and life-changing "prize," which seems nearly impossible to do.

6. I have to defeat powerful "bad guys" who have hurt and/or are threatening innocents.

7. I have to escape a terrible situation, which prevents me from living freely and happily.

8. I have to win over and/or hang on to a desired life partner, with whom I have a chance at my best life. But something is hugely in the way of that.

This list might seem limiting at first glance. Surely there are great stories that are about something other than these eight things, aren't there? I am not so sure. In my experience, honest analysis of favorite books, movies, plays, or series tends to reveal that one or more of these universally relatable challenges seem to always be at the heart of what's going on.

Likability

It really helps if we like the main character—if we see them as "good people." A lot of writers chafe at this idea. They cite darker, less likable characters in successful stories as examples of why this isn't a hard-and-fast "rule." And such characters seem more interesting. So let's talk about that.

Sometimes we don't exactly like the main character, in the traditional way, but we are so massively entertained, the stakes are so high, and/or they are being so relentlessly punished that we can forgive some unlikability. But the more unlikable they are, the more those other factors need to be in place.

Take *Scarface*, for instance. There are nearly constant life-and-death stakes. And though the main character becomes powerful fairly early (which can make it hard for audiences to stay invested, as we all love to root for the underdog), there are other people who are more power-ful, who threaten him. And his life spirals downward, just as he starts to reach the difficult and risky goals that we were intrigued to see him undertake. We might not like him, per se, but we are riveted in watching what's going on. Because what's at stake is crystal clear, incredibly primal, and easy to connect with emotionally. And it's massively entertaining in terms of action and suspense, in keeping with its genre.

Or take the series *House M.D.* The title character is very unlikable. But he's entertaining and fascinating to watch. He's also heroically saving lives every week, so we can somewhat forgive him for being a misanthrope who psychologically manipulates and abuses people. Not totally, but it helps us stay with him.

Imagine a show where a guy like Dr. House was not saving lives, and was not that entertaining or fascinating to watch but was still that mean. Say he worked in insurance and treated people that same way but was less witty, surprising, or outrageous. Or what if Tony Montana's life wasn't constantly at risk, with huge cinematic challenges closing in from every angle, in *Scarface*. Would we care enough to want to follow these guys? Or would we just think, "Why would I want to be with this person for two hours?"

This is the conscious or subconscious reaction that audiences (and professional readers) have to stories and story ideas more often than you might think. It all comes back to "Why should I care?" We have to give them a reason to care—to be emotionally invested in the main character and what they're dealing with.

It may be out of favor in certain circles to go for "lika-bility" with a main character, but in many genres, it's still essential. Take love stories. Here, the audience needs to root for two people to be together in the end. For this to work, the audience has to kind of fall in love with both the main character and their love interest, and feel that they are perfect matches for each other. If we don't strongly emotionally connect with the main character, will we really care about their love life? And if we don't agree with their choice of partner, will we care about them ending up together?

So how do you make the main character likable? There's one clear-cut area where a character's behavior will make the audience either like or dislike them: how they treat others. If they are really good to others, even to the point of forgoing their own interests at times, we will tend to instantly like them. If they are selfish and don't go out of their way for others, we will tend to not like them.

This is where the title of *Save the Cat!* comes from—it half-jokingly maintains that the main character needs to "save a cat" in the first ten minutes so we will want to engage with their story. But they can't just do something nice that's easy to do. They actually have to give up what they want, in some way, to help another. When they do that, we start to fall in love with them. When they do the opposite, and focus only on what they want, we tend to think, "Why would I want to follow this character? Why should I care about whatever they are going to face?" Selfishness can be poison in trying to make the audience stick with a main character.

In real life, there are a variety of ways in which people become more or less likable or interesting to us. But stories aren't real life, and the audience's relationship to the main character is a special and fragile one. To hook people into caring, this character usually has to be especially sympathetic and relatable. And if they aren't heroic or facing massive problems (and aren't incredibly fascinating/entertaining at all times)—then it's especially important that they are easy to bond with.

Even main characters who face life-and-death stakes are usually still depicted as pointedly sympathetic and likable in most commercially successful stories. Take *Star Wars* or *Harry Potter*. Their main characters deal with the highest possible stakes and are in heroic situations that are hugely entertaining to watch or read about—all things that can help make a less likable character more forgivable. And still their authors made them incredibly lovable, on top of that. Imagine these movies if the main characters were kind of selfish jerks, but still did all the heroic things and faced death, etc. Would these stories be as beloved?

Consider, as well, the main characters of the following movies:

- *I Am Legend*
- *Jerry Maguire*
- *The Nutty Professor*
- *12 Years a Slave*
- *Gravity*
- *The Graduate*
- *Austin Powers: International Man of Mystery*
- *The Sixth Sense*
- *Enchanted*
- *Meet the Parents*

There are a variety of genres here. But to my mind, all these main characters are presented in ways that make them extremely likable and relatable (albeit with relatable flaws). When in doubt, making the character easier to care about is generally worth doing. You almost can't err too much in that direction (unless the character becomes boring or unbelievable). But it's easy and common for writers to do the opposite—to present a main character who doesn't have a mix of qualities that truly engages a mass audience.

What about Character Arc?

Writers often create main characters that are not so likable—who are selfish and not good to others—with the idea that they will "arc" them to someone who learns to be nicer in the end. Because aren't main characters supposed to grow and change over the course of a movie?

It's true that the best stories often (but not always) tend to have a significant growth arc for the main character. In the end, they have somehow become a better version of themselves, as well as having solved some big problem in their world. And yes, this means they have to start the movie as the "not-best version of themselves."

But if the "not-best version" of your main character is a selfish jerk who hurts others in some way, readers will tend to not bond with them enough to want to stay with the story.

There are a rare handful of movies that are exceptions to this—and which successfully begin with a "jerk" main character. In these, the whole point is that a jerk becomes a better person, usually through some magical intervention. A great example is *Liar Liar*. The main character is purposefully presented as someone who is not particularly good to other people, because the whole point of the film is that a magic spell will force him to tell the truth and be better. That's the one time I think you can get away with the jerk opening. It's a rare exception. (*A Christmas Carol* is another example.)

But even in *Liar Liar*, you'll notice that Jim Carrey's character is actually really good to his kid, when he shows up. His problem is just that he's unreliable and evades the truth. But when present, he's a great, loving dad. So even in this movie about "a jerk who stops being a jerk," the filmmakers go out of their way to give him some positive qualities from the outset, in how he interacts with and loves his son.

Also, this character is *really* entertaining to watch, which helps a lot. The movie is hilarious from page one. And, importantly, he gets completely beaten up by life for most of the movie. They aren't life-and-death stakes, but he's under siege continuously, and it only builds. We can forgive bad behavior more easily when the main character is punished for it in a big way, and pretty much constantly.

Another example is *School of Rock*. Jack Black's character starts the movie behaving pretty selfishly. Although even then, he's an underdog who gets treated badly, which helps the audience get on his side. And he's also hilarious to watch. But the key is that the situation fairly quickly shifts from him merely exploiting the kids to the kids benefiting from what he's doing.

I like to think of the main character's flaw (and the thing we want to see them overcome, in their "arc") as the way they "get in their own way"—usually through limited thinking about what's possible for them. The flaw may have the side effect of constricting the good they can contribute to those around him or her, but they're usually not directly and actively hurting others in a way that we see on-screen and harshly blame them for. Instead, they're living a compromised version of what their life could be, because they somehow haven't risen up to face the internal blocks that keep them stuck. The big external challenge of the movie will force them to face this, often, and to make some changes. But they're not jerks!

Consider, for instance, the following main-character flaws:

- *Star Wars*—Luke doesn't believe in himself or trust the force.

- *Big*—Josh can't accept life as a kid.

- *It's a Wonderful Life*—George's ambitions for a big and successful life outside of Bedford Falls somewhat blind him to the blessings he has.

- *Working Girl*—Tess doesn't really believe in herself and the possibility of a better life/career beyond Staten Island.

- *Casablanca*—Rick doesn't believe in anything or pursue anything; he's just getting by and keeping his head down, staying uninvolved.

- *Lethal Weapon*—Riggs is suicidal due to the death of his wife.

- *Legally Blonde*—Elle has been living a sheltered life as a sorority princess, not trying to improve herself or be something more.

- *Field of Dreams*—Ray hasn't really made peace with his relationship with his late father.

- *Almost Famous*—William thinks rock stars are cool and wants their approval.

Notice a common theme? These characters are mostly relatable and even likable, but they aren't self-actualized and are clinging to smaller lives or ways of living (or fantasies) that don't ultimately serve them. They're not healthy and self-actualized in the most mature ways. And they need to grow—scary and difficult though it might be—in order to be their best, do their best, and contribute the most. Their arcs are about "living one's best life," not "learning to be good to other people."

In my experience, beginning writers tend to obsess too much about character arcs and flaws, and work too hard to give the main character too much room for growth, to the point where they start the movie rather unsympathetically. And this is hard to ever recover from.

I would also say that plenty of successful movies don't have major character arcs and flaws, with the main character having to significantly change to become much better or nicer in the end. Consider a handful of representative examples, across multiple genres:

- *Four Weddings and a Funeral*
- *Coming to America*
- *Stand and Deliver*
- *Get Out*
- *The Bourne Identity*
- *There's Something about Mary*
- *Say Anything . . .*
- *Die Hard*
- *Rear Window*
- *Erin Brockovich*

There are plenty of great stories where the main character is basically "good" all the way through, and though they grow in some ways, they don't substantially change at the end.

So, my advice is to not make "arc" the main priority, and especially don't start your character out hurting others in some way. A better way to address arc is to focus on what their best life would be, and why they don't have it. This tends to connect to some sort of "wound" that has led them to live life in a closed-down, less-than-ideal way—in terms of how they view themselves and what they think is possible.

The Goal of the Opening Pages

With any story idea, our main character has a starting point—a status quo life. It's hinted at in the logline and quickly described in the synopsis. And it's the main thing being depicted in the opening pages, before some "catalyst" event (aka "the inciting incident) introduces the main story problem.

These opening pages are crucial to hooking the reader into caring about the character. And they might be the only pages that get read. The script will likely be put down right away if those pages don't immediately engage the busy industry professional who has given it a chance by opening it.

Most screenwriters who have been at it for a while realize this, and try to pack some of their best description, dialogue, entertainment value, and overall scene writing into this crucial beginning section—which makes sense. There's also a common piece of advice that you should start the script *in medias res*, or "in the middle of things," meaning that something compelling, emotional, and filled with conflict and spectacle should happen right away.

I think this is a good idea, but that it's also crucial that writers fulfill the more important function of the script's opening, which is to establish relatability—to get readers understanding, interested in, and starting to emotionally invest in our main character, before hitting them with that catalyst event that rocks their world.

To achieve this, we have to introduce the character and their life at some length and in some breadth. This can take time. If we're mainly focused on trying to "grab" people with some huge event in the first few pages—or move around too much, introducing other characters—readers might find that they're not up to speed with the main character and their world enough, by the time of the catalyst, to really be able to engage. I see this problem very often in scripts.

It's not so much about "grabbing" the reader as it is drawing them into the world of the story, and its central figure, so they get intrigued and start to care. Any grabbing that's done—any exciting activity that we open in the middle of—should ideally just be the beginning of illustrating who this main character is, what their life situation is, and why readers should be intrigued by them. In other words, it's part of presenting their current status quo, before the catalyst rocks it.

One of the "grabbiest" movie openings happens in *Saving Private Ryan*, where we watch soldiers storming Omaha Beach. It's a harrowing and unforgettable sequence bringing to life the horrors of war. But if you really look at it in the context of what happens after, it is still merely setting up who Captain Miller is, and what he's been up to and dealing with, before the catalyst of getting the mission to go find Private Ryan. It's presenting an especially exciting version of his "status quo life," before the real story kicks in.

The first ten pages can be filled with fun-to-watch, high-conflict material, but I believe these should simply be examples of the kinds of things the main character is dealing with in their current normal life. Consider Ryan Reynolds working for hell-boss Sandra Bullock in *The Proposal*, Tom Cruise showing us his life as a sports agent who has grown a conscience in *Jerry Maguire*, or still-animated Amy Adams before she comes to New York City in *Enchanted*. This section should not already be challenging that status quo in a significant way. That should be saved for the catalyst. First, we have to compellingly dramatize what that status quo is, such that the reader is emotionally drawn in and beginning to care.

This means illustrating (not just talking about in dialogue) things like their living situation, occupation, social life, family and friends, and romantic relationships. It's about dramatizing how they spend their time, what their life is focused on, and who else is in it.

Knowing where the main character starts—and what we want to present about them to quickly get the audience up to speed—is key to understanding the idea, and is generally part of any pitch, no matter how brief. It's the jumping-off point.

And since the opening pages are so determinative to the rest of the script getting read, it's crucial that they engage the reader with the main character. This means almost immediately putting their most important feelings, life desires, and overall conflicts front and center and making them crystal clear. Ideally, the reader would be intrigued and entertained by them, liking them and even caring about them, before the catalyst sets the story in motion.

If we can deliver all of that in the first ten pages, they will keep reading.

Why We Care about Tony Soprano

In any story, in any medium, the audience needs a reason to connect with at least one character, to identify with what they're going through, and to get invested in their process of trying to resolve it. Television is no different.

But what if you're writing a dark drama centered on an antihero, as so many writers want to do these days? Well, the rules of "empathy" still apply. If the character isn't traditionally likable or sympathetic, then they at least need to be facing problems so big that the audience can't help but start to connect with them.

People often reference *Breaking Bad* as a show with a "dark" main character, but if you look at how the series began, Walter White was the most sympathetic person you could imagine—a loving husband and father and also a passionate chemistry teacher whose students didn't care, and who was underpaid, underappreciated, and diagnosed with a terminal illness. And as soon as he makes a critical decision to start cooking meth (to sympathetically provide money for his family, let's remember), he immediately places himself in enormous and constant jeopardy—his life will now be at risk, as well as his freedom. Also, his family could find out his horrible secret. It's hard to imagine a character with more to "root for" than this one. And all of that was necessary to balance out the fact that he was getting into a business that otherwise could seem completely unsympathetic to the audience.

Let's look at another example, which arguably kicked off this trend in earnest—HBO's groundbreaking *The Sopranos*, which Writers Guild members voted the best-written series of all time, in 2013. On the surface, Tony Soprano is unlikable: he's a violent mobster who also lies and cheats. But as he's introduced in the pilot, what we mostly see about him is that he is having panic attacks, feels scared, and is humiliated that he has to go to a therapist. Meanwhile, his own mother may be trying to have him killed. And he can't get the respect and peace he wants, from his wife, children, colleagues, or his life in general. His problems are a combination of really big and really relatable. Yes, on occasion he whacks a guy, but most of the show is about getting us inside his problem-filled life and personal, emotional perspective.

Another common technique is to surround an unlikable central character—like Michael Scott in the American version of *The Office*—with more relatable characters, like Jim and Pam. But even in that example, the so-called unlikable character was still made relatable and vulnerable in certain ways, so stories could be told from his point of view, where we are simultaneously shocked by his lack of self-awareness, which hurts others, but also at times sympathetic to the way he's trying to be loved and never getting what he wants.

Some comedies, like *It's Always Sunny in Philadelphia* or *Veep*, go further with making their characters hard to like. But these people are such underdogs, and the show punishes them so mercilessly (and they are so funny to watch), that we don't come away thinking, "I hate these despicable people and never want to watch them again." Actually, many viewers probably *do* feel that way, which limits these shows' reach somewhat, but most fans of the show don't actively hate the characters and respond to them as jerks. They more experience them as losers who get the crap kicked out of them, who desperately pursue selfish desires that never work out. If characters are always losing, and it's hilarious to watch them lose, we can forgive a lot.

On the other end of the spectrum, in terms of "likability," is a series like *Downton Abbey*—which found a way to get the audience to care about each member of a very large ensemble, by making them all pretty likable (though flawed). *Downton* had a couple of regular characters who would play a "bad guy" role at times, but even they got their humanity highlighted eventually, in stories of their own, which made the audience sympathize with what they were going through.

Somehow on this show, the audience consistently got why each of its huge cast of characters felt the way that they did and couldn't dismiss nearly anyone as truly unredeemable or the source of all the problems. Rather, the problems came from the complicated situations and agendas that the various people carried, which inevitably led to personal conflicts—where the audience understood and could feel for multiple parties in different ways.

Most series work this way—presenting a variety of relatable people who can "get stories" in any given episode and then intertwining those stories, with each new installment starting from scratch with new "crises of the week" (which are often connected to bigger ongoing problems). "Bad guys" are less useful to a TV writer than complicated and interesting people who have some human problem and desire that will forever torment them and help audiences to connect with them.

"Relatable" Checklist

If your idea can live up to this five-point mission statement, it should be "relatable" enough:

1. The main character will be so easy to like—and/or be so entertainingly besieged with problems—that the audience sympathizes. (On TV, this applies to the main character of each story in each episode.)

2. The main character's external life problems, in any story, are easy to identify with, on a primal, universal human level.

3. What they think, feel, and want will always be clear enough for the audience to share in their emotions and desires.

4. There will be a particular outcome of the story/episode that the audience will root for and feel something about.

5. If there's an arc of change (which series typically don't have), it's about the main character growing out of a limited version of themselves—not going from selfish to unselfish.

4

ORIGINAL

The most marketable story ideas tend to contain some intriguing conceptual hook at the heart of their premise and/or in their approach to a particular genre. To this extent, they're about something that we haven't quite seen before. They add something new—or do things in a new way—which makes them stand out.

At the same time, they observe certain storytelling and genre conventions that are necessary for the audience to buy in and engage. When those conventions are completely ignored or discarded for the sake of originality, things tend to fall apart quickly. It's a tricky balancing act, trying to figure out which "traditional" elements need to be there and which ones are fair game for innovation.

Some writers make originality their number one priority, without understanding or observing the other foundational aspects to a viable story idea or their genre. In looking to be different, they throw out the baby with the bathwater and come up with ideas that might be unique but don't have enough of these core qualities that are necessary to capture an audience.

One might assume newer writers would be more likely to copy what's already out there, and not be especially fresh or unique. But it's actually more common to see scripts from inexperienced writers fall short in the other six PROBLEM criteria—while focused on being "original."

This may be because writers tend to tire of what they see as a boring sameness to what's in the marketplace. They might decry all the sequels and other projects that seem to have gotten made because they were similar to something successful that came before. Creative people tend to want to push for something fresh, not see new variations on the same old thing. Critics—who have to watch everything and can become jaded by that—also tend to value originality extra highly. And both might decry what they see as too much "formula" out there.

This is an understandable impulse. But when something comes off as formulaic, it's not because it stuck to certain guidelines and principles that have been proven to be essential. It's because it did so in a way that seemed paint-by-numbers. In other words, the execution didn't elevate the material to something that seemed brand-new. And maybe the writer was too slavish to whatever formulaic elements they were using, to the point where the seams really showed. Maybe their concept fulfilled a classic, proven genre of some kind, but did so in ways that felt overly familiar, without adding anything special to it.

That's the key—creating something fresh and new, but within a somewhat familiar package—if the goal is to sell one's work. Because industry buyers, writers' representatives, and audiences don't value "newness" quite as highly as writers or critics. They tend to respond better to stories of a type they've seen before, with one big new and intriguing thing added. They aren't looking for writers to reinvent the wheel completely or to be different for the sake of being different.

It's easy to create something that's really "out-there" and doesn't fulfill foundational storytelling criteria. What's harder and more valued is to break fresh and intriguing ground within a tried-and-true genre, with a story that is not only "original" but also punishing, relatable, believable, life-altering, entertaining, and meaningful.

A Fresh Twist on the Familiar

Successful stories in any genre tend to give the audience the things they come to those genres for (action, comedy, romance, horror, etc.), but they do it in a way that seems original. So it helps to first study and understand the relevant genres and brainstorm ways to conceptually evolve from some of the best examples of it.

I once heard literary manager Victoria Wisdom give some great advice on this topic, which was this: build on successful movies in a genre, that you'd like to emulate, by adding or changing one key element of what has worked in the past. She used the example of how James Bond begat Jason Bourne (a spy who doesn't know he's a spy), and also *Mr. & Mrs. Smith* (about two spies who are married), which then led to *Spy Kids* (about two married spies whose kids become spies). Each was successful, and each was different enough from the others to feel like its own unique and special thing. And each observed the primary rules of the "spy movie" genre—and of story in general. The spies are on a mission with huge stakes and have a particular enemy they spend the whole movie fighting (in highly entertaining ways). They're overmatched by this villain and only able to defeat them in the very end. There's plenty of compelling action, and the audience emotionally bonds with the main character, and relates to and roots for them as they get punished on their way to an eventual breakthrough.

It helps to have a solid genre as a starting point—meaning a type of story that has worked many times for audiences. That way, a writer can build from a foundation that has certain PROBLEM elements inherent in it—which usually still need to be there in the new variation. In other words, if we think of the kinds of scenes and situations that tend to be in a successful spy movie (or whatever genre we're working in), we know that a successful new variation will probably need those, too. It just will be delivering them in original ways.

What doesn't work so well is when writers simply become test marketers who second-guess the audience and "what's currently in demand," and write only what they think will sell, or copy what's been successful without bringing some spark of intriguing uniqueness to it. A piece of writing needs its creator to have passion for it, and really love it, for it to come alive for readers. One generally can't create the next great and marketable anything if they don't personally believe in it and bring something of themselves to it that's fresh and new. The key is to mix one's own personal passions and creative tastes with knowledge of—and willingness to learn and work within—the fundamentals of story and genre.

Once a writer learns how to do this, and commits to it, they start focusing on the kinds of stories and projects that actually do have a fighting chance in the marketplace, if done well. And that's when the challenges of "originality" start to really become an issue. Because when we understand what makes an idea potentially sellable—and we focus only on generating ideas and writing stories that fit those criteria—we start to see that a lot of the things we come up with seem similar to things that have already been done. Meaning, they are not so original. The reason for this is that now we are eliminating 99 percent of what we might have tried to write about before we understood all this. It narrows the possibilities greatly.

This is a good thing, and a necessary step for a writer to get to, because it means they're no longer someone who doesn't truly understand story and genre and who can't work within them effectively. But they may start to look around at other examples within a certain genre, and feel that there isn't enough new territory for them. Every idea they come up with may seem too similar to examples of the genre in the past. After all, successful and capable writers have been racking their brains to come up with new variations on those same genres for decades. And now here they are, trying to do the same thing. That is where the real hard work of trying to be original within a viable framework begins.

I've witnessed this firsthand in the TV-development marketplace. Every year, the major networks will tell the big agencies (who tell their writer clients) what they are "looking for," meaning what kinds of new show ideas they want to be pitched. Inevitably, on the one-hour-drama side, these "network needs" will include fresh and original examples of staples like the cop show, the medical show, and the legal show. These three genres have worked over and over on television, so they know they want more of them. But for an idea to go the distance, it has to carve out fresh territory that hasn't quite been seen before.

Now, one might look at what's on TV and say that there are a lot of similar cop shows. But if we ignore spin-offs and franchises, for a moment, and look only at original show ideas that were successful, they usually did something different from all shows that came before. Something about the cops, the unit, the cases, and/or how they work on them was fresh—even while the basic genre elements remained basically the same.

How many unique variations on a "cop show" can there be, in the end? Especially if we accept that the cases have to be really high stakes (like murders) and solved by the end of an episode? Well, that's the question hungry TV writers ask themselves every year as they work to come up with ideas for their own new cop show, and try to sell them to the networks. Hundreds of new ideas are pitched, but only a handful will ever make it on the air. And this is from seasoned professional TV writers. It isn't easy.

This same challenge holds true in every genre and medium where writers seek to tell stories. Inevitably, others have already taken what seems like every possible new idea for our genre, our topic, and our type of story. So, what are we going to do? Sometimes the answer could be to blend two genres in a way that delivers the expectations of one or both of them really effectively, but in a new way. Consider "vampires" meets "teen romance" in *Twilight*. In other cases, it can be about finding some fresh type of challenge, liability, conflict, or difficulty that could add further complications to the main character's situation. Since we're always looking for more of those things, that's a good place to start.

There's Another Project Just Like Mine!

It's almost inevitable that with anything we write, someone else has written or is writing something similar, in terms of concept, subject, and/or setting. There are only so many ideas and types of premises out there that can fit the criteria for a winning story, and only so many kinds of human experiences to base a story on, so it's a common occurrence to find out that our piece isn't as unique, special, fresh, and new as we might have hoped it was. (Even if it's based on a specific true story.) And sometimes, other projects we hear about that are similar are much further along toward being produced and have much bigger names behind them.

It's normal to despair in this situation and to feel that it renders all our hard work a waste. But that's not usually true, and all is not lost. There are several reasons why this incredibly frequent state of affairs is not cause for panic:

1. Most movie and TV projects—even the ones that big-name writers are being paid to write—never get produced, or if they do, they don't reach a large audience. The people we send our work to likely haven't seen them or aren't familiar with them. Even when news stories make it seem as though a competitive project is on the fast track toward success, there's usually more to the story, and very often, nothing ever comes of them, or at least nothing significant.

2. Anything we write when we're not yet a well-established, successful writer is likely to serve only as a "writing sample" and won't get produced

anyway. At best, it might do well in contests, win us a manager or agent, and/or get us meetings with producers who become "fans" of our work. But typically, they can't or won't do anything with this script that made them a fan. They just really want to see the next thing we write. This happens constantly.

3. And this is considered a best-case scenario. Most scripts for most writers don't achieve any of these things. But if a piece of writing does, it probably won't matter that it's similar to something else that has beaten it to the marketplace. Because they're judging us by our writing and storytelling ability, and what we did with our concept, and how we made it ours. They're looking at it as a sample that shows them whether we're a writer they might want to be in business with moving forward. No writer wants to hear that, and with every project, we really hope we can sell it and get it produced, but the real chances of that happening are always tiny.

4. On the rare occasion that the competitive project does go the distance and gets made and is successful and well-known, and our project also gets to a place where people might seriously consider producing it,

the marketplace often has room for more than one project with similar subjects or concepts. Remember *Deep Impact* and *Armageddon*? Both came out in 1998. How about *18 Again!*, *Vice Versa*, and *Big*? All three were adult-child body-switching movies, and all were released in 1988. Or consider *Christopher Columbus: The Discovery* and *1492: Conquest of Paradise*. Both were about Columbus, and both came out in 1992.

We might then ask, "What if another project out there is exactly the same as mine, to the point where the two could not coexist?" Well, that is incredibly rare. But it is possible that another project is so close to ours, and ahead of ours in every way, that people could look at ours and think it's basically the same thing or a knockoff, and thus not original enough.

As unlikely as that is to happen, here's what we can do when we hear about such a potential project, whether it's in development or already released: research it, and try to read and/or watch it.

This is the opposite of what I've seen many writers do in this situation. Instead, they say something like, "I purposefully avoided finding out too much about it, because I didn't want to be influenced by it." I disagree with that approach. If our concern is that this other project is too close to ours, wouldn't we want to make sure? And perhaps have the opportunity to adjust ours so that is no longer the case? No one's going to give us credit for "accidentally being the same, because we never saw it, meaning we didn't consciously copy it," so what's the point of avoiding it?

Most of the time, when we check out the competitive project(s), we find that although there are some similarities, they have a different focus in certain key ways. And we can also learn from what we don't think works or don't like about their approach, and make sure we don't make those same mistakes. It actually tends to solidify our sense of what we wanted to do, and usually that is different enough from what they did that it can give us a shot in the arm to check theirs out. It helps us to identify what's uniquely interesting about our idea and what we want to focus on. We can work to carve out our unique territory even further so that what we create is clearly significantly different from any apparent "competition."

Writer's "Voice" and Dealing with Feedback

Originality is not just about having an idea with a fresh, new, sellable hook. It's about one's view of the world and of people, and how that is communicated within an idea or piece of writing.

New writers are highly valued when they seem to have a unique and memorable "voice," where readers come away thinking, "Wow, this writer is one of a kind," or "Nobody else could have written this, in this way, but this person." There's a singularity to the writer's point of view and way of expressing it. The way their brain works and how that comes out on the page is appealingly unique to them.

One key way that "voice" comes out is through characters. Do they feel like real and authentic, one-of-a-kind human beings, different from everyone else on Earth? (The way we all are.) Are they super specific, down to the fine detail? And can their particular qualities be really memorable and entertaining to watch? Can they defy stereotypes and do and say things that only they could do or say? If so, they will feel like original creations.

Some aspects of "voice" come from what a writer chooses to focus on and the level of intriguing detail they can bring forth in whatever and whoever it is they write about. This can stem from writing about one's own experience. Or it can come from research. The more we can make our writing feel well observed and real but also memorable and unique to us, the more people will think we have a great "voice."

One can't force a voice. It's something that comes out of them with practice and experience. They will tend to write about certain kinds of people and situations, in certain types of ways, that is unique to them. So, it's helpful to notice and trust in our obsessions. Notice what we're uniquely interested in, and listen to that. Follow that (while, of course, also making sure to follow these other guidelines).

It's easy to get talked out of one's own "voice" by well-meaning others when they give feedback. Some writers will note others' lukewarm reactions and decide that these reactions are 100 percent right, that it's "not good enough," or that they're "not good enough"—instead of trusting that there is something in their unique ideas, interests, and passions that can really work and be successful if they follow it. It can be easy to get talked out of something that, with more work, could be viable material. And notes are often about someone else's personal tastes. I am especially cautious about adopting others' helpful "fixes" to problems they can't quite articulate. Better to learn what they think the problems are, decide if I agree, and address them in my own voice.

On the other hand, many writers make the opposite mistake, and are too closed off to any notes. They might write off everyone's feedback as being "really about them" (and "them not getting my voice") and refuse to change much of anything. This usually means the writer isn't thinking enough about the audience they're trying to serve and seeing these first readers as representatives of that potential audience. It can be very valuable to get "notes" on material, especially ones that address the seven elements in this book and that come from multiple honest people whose opinion on such things are worthy of trust. A consensus on what the problems seem to be is very useful.

As with so many things, it's about finding a balance—where we are boldly willing to hear what others have to say and to rethink our work in significant ways, if needed—without letting go of what makes it potentially special, original, and uniquely "us."

Why They Make Bad Movies

Beginning screenwriters are often shocked to hear how competitive the field is and how difficult it is to break in. They think their chief problem is that it's a closed industry. It can't be that it's so difficult and rare to create something that impresses the gatekeepers. If only the writers with the very best skill, craft, artistry, and ideas are able to sell their material or get hired, how does that jibe with the fact that there's so much "crap" that gets made by

Hollywood? And this "crap" they're talking about tends to especially fail, in their eyes, in terms of originality.

It's a common and reasonable question, but it's based on making the mistake of conflating two very different events. The first is a new writer getting noticed and moving ahead in their career in some way. (Which of course is every new writer's hope.) The second is a movie getting green-lit to production and ultimate release. These two things happen totally separately from each other and are based on almost completely different factors.

Let's start with the new writer getting noticed. What does it take for this to happen? Simple: a single script (in TV or film) that really stands out and impresses the people who evaluate, develop, and/or sell screenwriting for a living (managers, agents, producers, and certain executives at the studios and networks). Those folks are looking for new material and new writers. But they don't need a huge number of them, and they have to wade through literally hundreds of scripts they feel don't work to find even one that might.

What are they looking for? A fresh idea they think could sell, backed by a very well-executed script. And just as importantly, they want distinctly original voices from writers who have mastered the fundamentals and can produce on the page at a professional level that is compelling, clear, believable, entertaining, emotionally involving, and a true pleasure to read.

That's not easy to achieve, and most people who try their hand at screenwriting never get there. Those who do have usually worked very hard and long on many scripts for many years and educated themselves hugely along the way. Their first goal is to simply get represented and develop interest in their work from within the industry. That's what their scripts are geared to do (unless they're looking to make the movie themselves, independently).

On the other end of the process, the one where movies are getting green-lit to production, you have executives looking to package existing projects with stars and directors in order to release them as a commercial product. Let's look at the factors that play into these decisions and that might result in the "bad" movies that make it seem like writers don't have to be "good" to make it in Hollywood.

First, understand that the film industry is a business like any other, meaning that the only goal of the decision makers who green-light movies is to make a profit. If they don't consistently do that, they're out of business. Whether they personally think what they're making is "good" or "original" or not, and whether they'd love to see it, is largely irrelevant. A lot of these people are smart, educated, worldly types who might personally prefer the same kind of movies that a typical screenwriter might respect. They're just not personally obsessed with the creative/artistic side of things, as writers often are, and they won't make such movies if they don't seem like they will be profitable.

What makes a script or idea for a movie a good choice from a businessperson's perspective? Obviously, they want the largest number of people to consume it, based on what they've seen audiences buy in recent years. It's not an exact science, because any supposed "sure thing" can end up not working with audiences. But you only have to look at the top-grossing movies to see that prior brand awareness and popularity is a key element. And this can run counter to the priority of "originality."

It's much easier to get a distracted population with so many entertainment options to understand, recognize, and be interested in something that's connected to material they already know. It just makes business sense. We don't have to like it, and it might lead to a seeming paucity of "good movies" (or startlingly original ones), but it seems to be the economic reality.

Paul Blart: Mall Cop 2 may be a failure in terms of reviews, but it still brought in $108 million in worldwide box office, on a budget of $30 million. That might not be a big hit, but the first *Paul Blart* made $183 million on a budget of $26 million. From a business perspective, that's sound decision making.

Very smart people study these things extremely seriously. It doesn't mean they don't guess wrong at times; of course they do. But they likely had solid business/economic reasons behind what they did. And those reasons always trump whether a movie is "good" or not.

Another thing to understand is that no one sets out to make unoriginal crap (unless they know it will still make tons of money regardless). They set out to make something that will provide audiences with the types of emotional experiences and entertainment that have proven to be successful in the past. It's just really hard to make something that works, in any genre. It's a rare thing. A lot of elements have to come together well, almost like lightning in a bottle. It's much more normal to make a bad or mediocre movie (just as it is to write a bad or mediocre script) than to truly succeed, either commercially or in terms of "quality."

None of this has much to do with the other end of the process, where aspiring writers are trying to break in. Writers almost never break in with a green-lit movie. Rather, breaking in means impressing a manager, an agent, or a producer with a script that likely won't even sell, let alone get made, but that puts them on the radar of the industry, gets them fans, and starts to give them some momentum toward future sales or employment.

You might ask yourself, did the writers of "bad movies" actually make it to the top of the heap at some point, bypassing all the other aspiring writers at the time, with something that completely impressed people as unique and great?

The answer is almost always yes.

This "bad movie" you're now seeing might be bad for all sorts of reasons that don't have to do with their individual writing contribution. But even if it does, you're probably looking at a professional writer who has written many, many screenplays and gradually worked their way up with some very impressive work that ultimately led to their employment on the bad movie. It's possible that they worked on the bad movie mainly for the money, and it wasn't the best medium for showcasing their talents. Or the development process could've been rushed. There was also very likely a variety of writers employed on it, with the final product a hodgepodge of their different contributions. There might've been difficulty reaching a version that equally pleased director, studio, and star with a single, solid creative vision that worked. The financing company might have even (perhaps rightly) recognized that a great script wasn't absolutely key to the film's business prospects.

Or it could have just been a flawed approach to a movie that the writer either came up with or had forced on them by someone else.

But make no mistake, virtually any writer credited on even a bad movie has gone far past the basic screenwriting fundamentals that vex 99 percent of beginning writers and has written at least one "great" script that proved they "had it." They aren't simply bad writers who could easily be replaced by the average aspiring writer who has taken a class and written a script or two.

My advice is to recognize and respect the challenge of rising to the level that would allow one to start a professional career. And realize that the bad movies you see in theaters don't mean that it should be easy. It isn't—not because the industry is so closed, but because it's hard to do this really well.

In Judd Apatow's book *Sick in the Head*, Jerry Seinfeld commented on the nature of great comedians. He might as well have been talking about screenwriting when he said, "That's the greatest thing about comedy. If you've got talent, it's unmistakable. No one misses it and you don't have to wait around for a break. It's very easy to get a break. It's very hard to be good enough."

Doctors, Lawyers, and Cops

Buyers of TV are always looking for something unique and original, but as in other media, what works best is a fresh twist on a proven genre, where a writer who clearly understands how certain types of shows work (usually from having been a staff writer of such shows) manages to masterfully observe and execute those fundamentals while applying them to something brand-new that hasn't quite been seen before.

I used to lament the fact that so many drama series focus on some variation of cops, lawyers, and/or doctors. I tried pitching and developing multiple series about other kinds of workplaces, which usually failed. I felt, like many aspiring television writers do, that there are a multitude of different kinds of job challenges that could make for compelling television.

But in my years of doing it professionally—selling some ideas but having many others batted down by executives, producers, or my own agents—I learned some things. And one of the chief lessons is that we don't want to create a show where the story challenges center on "work responsibilities," unless it's for some variation on one of those golden three occupations.

The kind of jobs that can drive the bulk of the stories on a successful series generally have three specific qualities:

1. They are heroic: they involve doing something for others. The show's regulars are involved in protecting, helping, and/or fighting for humanity, beyond their personal sphere.

2. The stakes are sky-high. If they fail, people die, murderers go free, innocent people get life in prison, etc.

3. The nature of their work consists of entertaining-to-watch scenes of compelling interpersonal confrontations, with high emotions and high stakes for all.

Law & Order is perhaps the quintessential example of this. A unique (at its time) hybrid of "investigative/police" show and "legal/courtroom" show, it focused on professionals fighting on behalf of society and crime victims to identify who committed a murder and bring them to justice.

The process of achieving that goal is made up entirely of high-conflict, high-stakes, high-emotion confrontations with witnesses, suspects, bosses, opposing counsel, judges, and juries. Every scene, on the best episodes, is a fun-to-watch attempt to solve the larger story problem of the episode (the murder), in which the law-enforcement characters meet resistance and/or force revelations, which then require further action on their part—leading to more scenes.

Over the years, audiences have consistently shown that they enjoy watching the procedure of various kinds of police, lawyers, and doctors doing their jobs—for these reasons. So networks always want more of them, albeit with fresh variations. There have also been successful shows about other kinds of heroic adventurers, whose job or role in society involves fighting against dangers on behalf of others—such as *Buffy the Vampire Slayer*, *Alias*, *The Walking Dead*, and *Star Trek*. These shows meet the same criteria as the classic three "procedural" show occupations, where the audience is mainly concerned with solving the "case of the week."

Many one-hour dramas feature this kind of story "franchise." It's an endlessly repeatable way to generate stories—they walk in the door, so to speak, as this week's problem or case. Series that don't have a procedural story generator have to rely on the personal lives of their series regulars for all the conflict and problems. In these shows (which include all comedies and perhaps half the dramas on television), the central problem, goal, and stakes of an episodic story typically matter only to its main character. They're usually not heroic, and it's not about workplace success. They're personal.

Writers often decide to create shows set at some other kind of workplace and make the story challenges about "work stuff." They might reason that there have been successful shows about all sorts of other professions: Ad agency executives. High school football coaches. Sketch-comedy-show writer-producers. Certainly, the challenges of working at these occupations have been the foundation for successful television series. Right?

On the surface, it might seem that way. But there's a key difference. The stories on episodes of these shows don't focus primarily on job-related assignments and difficulties, unless they lead to engaging challenges in the characters' personal lives. The audience isn't meant to be invested in the characters simply succeeding in a work task over the course of the episode the way they would with doctors, lawyers, cops, or starship captains. The stakes just aren't high enough, and the process of doing most jobs isn't entertaining to watch (or sympathetic), in the same way that the "heroic" jobs are.

Nobody wants to watch scene after scene of Don Draper on *Mad Men* wrestling with an ad campaign as the episode's "A Story"—with the climax of the episode being the campaign's success. The same is true about Liz Lemon creating an episode of *TGS*, a fictional *SNL* analogue on *30 Rock*. The minutiae of their work, and its goals, are not why we watch. It's about the characters and their personal life challenges. We are invested in the characters personally, and we care about the high stakes they face in their own lives. And so, their "workplace challenges" are merely a backdrop that serves to generate conflicts and problems that will affect these characters on a personal level. But there's no heroic mission to invest in. What the audience cares about instead are these individuals' frustrations in their personal lives, their fantasies of what they wish their lives could be, the challenges of trying to get them there, and the high-stakes personal crises and conflicts that come up in the process.

"Original" Checklist

If your idea can live up to this five-point mission statement, it should be "original" enough:

1. My story/series honors the foundational principles of a viable genre but adds something intriguingly brand-new.

2. The central problematic situation (and my logline) has an easily understandable "hook" that strongly intrigues.

3. There's something within it I am passionate about, that is uniquely me in some way, that will come through as part of my "voice."

4. There is enough that is different about the concept compared with other similar well-known projects.

5. My key characters are specific and one of a kind in intriguing ways that elevate the story beyond the familiar.

5
BELIEVABLE

Stories are generally about exaggerated situations—not normal life, with all its boring "realness." Even in the most grounded of genres, we need to find something that will entertain the audience and get them strongly emotionally invested. This requires "punishing" characters who are "relatable" in some "original" way that is "life-altering," "entertaining" to watch, and "meaningful."

In our quest to do those things, we step into a minefield in which, at every turn, we're tempted to write something that isn't really believable.

"Audiences will go with us," we assure ourselves. I mean, after all, they've accepted "body-switch" movies and people breaking into song in the middle of scenes, as well as countless variations of zombies, aliens, and/or vampires. Clearly, they're willing to suspend disbelief and accept whatever we throw at them, right?

Unfortunately, it's not that easy.

Yes, it's possible to get the audience to take a leap at the beginning of a movie. Usually they'll only willingly take one such leap, and it has to be clearly set up and offered to them in such a way that they go, "Okay, this Zoltar machine is magical, and it turned this kid into an adult Tom Hanks," or, "The world these characters know is really a computer-generated matrix created by machines who use people as batteries," or, "Wizards are real, and there's a school for them." If it's carefully set up and explained through some reasonable-seeming mechanism in the first 10–15 percent of the narrative, then there's a chance they'll accept it.

But from that point on, the writer's job is to explore the situation in the most believable way possible. In other words, characters should do and say things that most people would do or say in that situation if they were them. Everything that happens should be understandable and make sense, in a grounded, real-life way, according to the character agendas and situational challenges that have been laid out. Yes, there may be something (usually only one major thing) that's big and outrageous and different from most people's normal lives, but beyond that, it should all feel *real*.

One of the most common reasons readers don't want to continue with a script—or don't want to read it after seeing a brief synopsis—is that something about what's happening doesn't feel real. They don't believe people would do or say what this piece of writing is making them do or say. Or they just don't "get" the concept and buy into it based on the writer's explanation of it (or maybe the writer didn't provide enough of an explanation, which is also a common occurrence).

The point of creating an outrageous situation to put relatable characters in is to then explore what real people would do in that situation. That's what the audience connects with. If the way everything works doesn't make total sense to them—or if the things people do don't come across as real, understandable, and believable—then they quickly, and often permanently, check out. They may not even be conscious of the reason. All they know is they're not invested.

On the other hand, the more real, specific, and understandable things are—and the more people behave in completely believable ways, given the situation and what they want—the more fascinated audiences tend to get.

That's especially true if all the other PROBLEM elements are also in place.

Zombies, Aliens, and Vampires

When a story proposes something fantastical and different from our normal world, it really helps if it's connected to something audiences have seen and accepted before and that has a place in popular culture already. That's why there are so many variations on zombie, alien, and vampire stories. (And a few other fantasy tropes.) It's much easier to present a fresh variation on one of these tropes than to try to get an audience to understand and buy into some completely made-up and brand-new world of beings that have just been created for this project. It's really tough to get across one's own brand of fantastical creature or situation that isn't already understood by audiences due to their lack of past exposure to it. While it might seem like the story would earn points for originality, what tends to happen is readers thinking, "I don't buy it." Or even worse: "I don't understand."

Readers have to understand what's going on before they can even decide whether it's believable or compelling. And "I don't understand" is a very common response to scripts, especially when they deal with elaborate fantasy or science fiction premises, or otherworldly supernatural creatures and realms. And it makes for what might be the single most unpleasant experience a reader can have: being confused.

Never Confuse

"Don't bore them" might be the cardinal rule of any dramatic writing, but "don't confuse them" is equally important, because when we confuse people as a writer, they start to get angry with us. If they don't get what's going on (especially when we combine that with them not really buying into things as real), they will put down the script in a hurry. Or if they're forced to read on, they will do so with irritation.

This happens often—and not just with fantasy concepts. Screenwriters often confuse readers when they neglect to convey necessary information, because they're so concerned with not writing blatantly expositional dialogue—the kind where people woodenly and unbeliev-ably speak information to one another that everyone already knows, because the audience needs to know it. Most writers learn early on to avoid that like the plague. But what some do is err in the opposite direction, and have their characters talk about people and situations that the audience doesn't know enough about to be able to follow what's going on, making them feel like they're on the outside looking in. This tends to alienate readers just as much.

Somehow screenwriters have to walk the difficult tightrope of telling the audience everything they need to know—so they can process and understand what's happening and being discussed—without being obvious about it. This is why simple story concepts tend to work better than complicated ones—because there is only so much information a writer can download to a reader in an effective fashion and have the reader absorb and accept it all and be compelled to follow what's happening.

This is true even when "exposition" is handled in the ideal way, which involves "showing" instead of "telling." What this means is that if we want an audience to understand any facts about a character or situation in our story, we have to do it within compelling dramatic (or comedic) scenes, where that information becomes obvious to the reader because of what's happening in the scene—not from someone speaking it in dialogue.

Simple example: We want the audience to know two people are married. We don't have anyone say that in dialogue. We show the two in a situation that makes it clear that they're married—living in the same house, sleeping together, interacting with their shared kids, etc. (Or even actually getting married.) We can never take for granted that the audience will just understand even such simple things. We can't just describe a character as another character's husband in description—because the viewing audience doesn't get to read the description. (And the description should be only what the audience would see and understand from what they're seeing.) If the audience needs to know it, we have to lead them by the hand and explicitly illustrate all of it.

It's helpful, then, to limit the number of facts the audience needs to understand. If every fact requires some scene or moment that demonstrates that fact to the audience, it can add up to a lot of beats that are hard to string together dramatically and make compelling. So, if our idea has a lot of complicated backstory that the audience needs to understand, early in the script, in order to comprehend what's going on, we may need to simplify the concept.

This issue can really cause difficulty for some writers who are especially interested in elaborate fantastical world building, perhaps more so than connecting with the audience on an emotional level. "World building" only works when the information readers have to understand to enjoy the story is fairly simple and clear, and the story works on a primal, emotional, human level, first and foremost.

How Is the World Different from Ours?

Whenever a story is set in a world where something is not the same as the world we all live in now, it's important to define all the dissimilar elements quickly, at the beginning. (This also applies to the beginning of any pitch, logline, or query.) When someone hears or reads a story idea and sees that it has some fantastical elements to it—or is set in the future or anywhere different from "Earth in the present" as we know it—they tend to want to know, right away, exactly what these differences are. They must feel that they "get" the world and its rules before they're able to process anything else.

Successful stories usually make it their first priority to answer any potential questions and define all the "rules" right out of the gate. By "rules" I mean the ways things work in this different world, including any special beings or powers and what the limitations and parameters of those are. The rules must be quickly put into a form that anyone can understand and accept and not have a million questions about (or have trouble buying into completely) so that they can enjoy the story that follows.

Writers of such stories sometimes become so used to the elements they made up that they take them for granted and don't realize how much explanation is necessary for the rest of us to buy in. Ideally these elements would be fairly simple, clear, and easy to understand and believe. Some writers have a tendency to create complicated, convoluted, and hard-to-understand situations and fail to explicitly clarify up top how everything works. To them, all that they have created is easy to get, even self-evident—but to the reader it can seem beyond comprehension.

Sometimes writers try to parcel out information over the course of a script, not realizing how important it is for the audience to fully grasp everything that's different about the story's world at the beginning in order to have any hope of emotionally connecting with it. If they don't understand the rules, and who is in this world, and what they want, and what's in the way, and how it all works—and how it contrasts with our world—they usually can't find a way "in," where they relate to the characters and what's happening on a human level.

And that's ultimately the goal. The audience enjoys watching relatable human beings, behaving in relatable ways while faced with a punishing challenge. They aren't inherently interested in the fantastical world itself—at least, the majority of them aren't—and neither are producers, agents, publishers, etc. They're interested in how the fantastical elements impact people who are basically a lot like us, and how these elements create goals and difficulties that *anyone* can relate to. So the best scenarios center on a relatively simple and easy-to-understand situation (even if it's fantastical) explained quickly so that we can then get into the important part—the story.

The general rule is that we get one, and only one, big buy-in from the audience, in terms of the story taking place in a world different from ours in some way. Maybe the zombie apocalypse has happened. Or aliens have come to Earth. Or there are vampires in our high schools. The audience can accept that one fantastical thing as long as we make it clearly understandable. But after that, everything else that happens has to involve people behaving the way real people would behave in that situation. It's great to put relatable people in extraordinary circumstances, but then they have to say and do things that a real person would say or do, from that point forward.

But lest you think all this only applies to writers of science fiction, fantasy, and the like, the same principles hold true in every genre, including the most grounded dramas and comedies.

Almost every successful story's "hook"—which is meant to inspire readers to want to escape into watching or reading it—has something in it that could be hard to buy if it's not handled carefully. It's important that we understand what that might be, in our story and basic concept, and that we work to make sure that the average person can buy it. Because that's ultimately our audience—the average person, whom we hope to make feel something with our work.

Going for "the Real"

Beyond just being understandable, we want to make sure that all the elements of our premise really add up, in the audience's mind, so that they can say, "Yes, I can see all that happening. I can understand why these characters would do what you're saying they do, given their situation. I get how what's going on could happen, and how it could present the kind of challenge you're describing." Earning that acceptance on the part of readers tends to be tougher than it looks.

For instance, in the world of comedy, it's funny when things are exaggerated beyond what's normal and reasonable, usually in terms of human behavior, emotions, and characteristics. Take any episode of *Will & Grace* or *30 Rock*. The characters tend to embody exaggerations of certain qualities; and their situations, desires, and ways of acting and speaking tend to be, well, funnier than average, in a consistent way. But the people still feel real, in terms of what's driving them and their behavior. Exaggerated, but still real.

But what happens when you're watching a comedy and people do or say things that you don't really believe any real person in that situation would ever do or say? You don't laugh. Not only do you not laugh, you might start to get upset with the writer for trying to manipulate you into laughing with such blatant unreality. It might start to make you check out of what you're watching. This is what we call "over-the-top"—when something just feels too unbelievable. The best comedy is grounded in relatable human behavior. Yes, the situations and characters are somewhat exaggerated, but only somewhat. Ultimately, they behave the way you and I might, faced with the situation they're in, if we were them.

When plotting out the idea for a story (or specific scenes), it's always a good practice to check in with each character and make sure everything they're doing comes from a "real" place. Where are they at, at this present moment? What do they want? What's in the way? What do they feel? What do they want to do? What would happen if they tried to do it? Ideally everything people do and say stems from believable answers to these questions.

When in doubt, stick with what actual people would do in that situation. This is how characters start to feel real to the audience. (It also makes it easier for actors to believably play them.) Don't go first for the comedy, or the spectacle, or the action, or the coolness. In this sense, being entertaining takes a back seat to being believable and relatable. Hopefully the basic premise, characters, and situations fit an identifiable genre that has elements that will prove entertaining. That way it's safe to start with what is "grounded"—meaning what's real.

When a writer sends me a logline or short query/ synopsis for a script they've been working on, I often have believability questions that get in the way. They have characters making decisions and taking actions that don't seem to make complete sense from the character's point of view, given their situation. In the rush to come up with an idea that intrigues and entertains, that meets a certain genre, and that sounds fresh and original, writers can take shortcuts, where they don't really ask themselves, "Would this character *really* do what I have them doing here, when faced with this situation?" If the answer is anything less than "I can totally see them doing it," there is probably more work to be done. Professional readers will always ask that question. They might not ask it consciously, but as soon as characters start behaving in ways that don't meet this test, it will become an issue.

When coming up with an idea, one has to really think through the perspectives of all the key characters, and make sure they're all operating in ways that are easy to "buy." This means exploring each character at some depth and asking, "What might they do in this situation? What would make them do this? How do their situation and desires push them into this? What do they think is going to happen when they do this? How do they believe doing this would serve their goals?"

This can be especially important with "villain" characters. Not every type of story has to have one main antagonist, but whoever provides strong difficulties for the main character needs motivations for their actions that make sense to the audience. Whether the oppositional force is more of an institution or a government or a creature, whoever is making the key decisions will ideally be driven by something that the audience can relate to and buy into, even if they don't agree with the decisions and want the villain to lose. Even if the villain is motivated by greed, sadism, lust for power, etc., their actions still have to make logical sense on a human level.

God and the Devil Are in the Details

In going for "realness," we're not just trying to meet a minimum level, one where audiences think what's going on seems plausible enough. One of the keys to writing something that gets noticed, and can advance a career, is to achieve a level of detailed specific realness that wows people as authentic and original, because the writer seems to understand their people, settings, and activities, and can bring that to life vividly and memorably on the page. When achieved in tandem with the other PROBLEM elements, this extraordinary level of realness can make a script stand out in a big way.

This means we're looking for the detail, especially in terms of character and behavior. God is in the details, right? They also say the devil is in the details. Because it's not easy to create people that seem so specific and real. It's much easier to write characters who are vague types, pawns of the author who only exist to go through certain actions in the face of created story challenges.

Part of the writer's role is to look for the interesting details that are not what one might expect, and which, because they're unexpected, actually feel more real, somehow. In real life, people aren't vague types. They are bundles of contradictions. They can be sympathetic and loathsome, loving and sadistic, vulnerable and cool. So should characters be. This is what makes them feel "three-dimensional," instead of "one-dimensional," a term often used to critique characters.

Is there room for one-dimensional characters in some roles, in some genres? Perhaps. Not every character has to be treated with such complexity and depth. But for the most important characters, a story feels much richer, more interesting, and more real when the audience is able to see the complicated humanity within them and relate on some level to it—even though the character, on its surface, might be very different from them.

Forced to Coexist

Television series operate under the same constraints as other story forms, in terms of everything needing to seem "real." No matter how "out-there" the central situation seems to be (with zombies, aliens, vampires, or other fantasy elements), a good show is ultimately about relatable people dealing with the situation in ways that make sense and are easy to buy into.

And the same principles apply in terms of overall series concept. One can generally get away with a single fantastical leap in a premise, but only if it's clearly explained and easy to understand and accept—at the very beginning of the pilot (and the beginning of the writer's pitch for the series). Convoluted concepts with no familiar elements are usually the writer's enemy. The goal is to get people buying in quickly so they can relax into engaging with the characters and story problems, which are going to stem from whatever singular difficult situation the series is based on.

There's another area where "believability" comes up in television. Because series are about a web of characters in conflict, and certain problematic circumstances they all share, the characters need a believable, organic reason why they will be constantly in one another's lives, and be affected by the same things, indefinitely.

This might seem like an obvious point, but series ideas struggle when they don't have a mechanism for this that makes logical sense. If the series regulars all work together in the same location, or are in the same family, or live together (or close to one another), or are close friends who get together constantly, then they have such a reason.

But what if they don't?

Ideas that aren't about coworkers, family, neighbors, and/or friends can have a hard time making sure that the characters are continually interacting and dealing with the same set of problems. And a show can easily fragment into what seems like separate shows about separate people with their own separate lives who rarely interact with one another. And this usually doesn't work so well.

Writers occasionally pitch shows about a group of people who aren't really going to be constantly in scenes together—like a show set in a certain industry, in a certain city, where nobody works in the same exact place together. They might have some common experiences, but if they aren't friends, family, neighbors, or working in the same room together a lot, how will the scenes and stories feature this ensemble as a cohesive unit?

Even if the characters all live in the same building, if they don't share common spaces and aren't super close friends who choose to be together, they're not forced to coexist (and deal with the conflicts inherent in that), the way TV characters usually are. This is one of the reasons why it's hard to make shows work when they're set at a college or university. College students have much more freedom of movement and separation from other people, compared with high school students—who are trapped both in school every day with the same people and in a home with their families. There's only one cafeteria where everyone eats lunch, and one dinner table at home. For teenagers, there's no escape. Which is great for drama (or comedy).

If the series regulars aren't forced by their situations to be in physical proximity, on a very regular basis, for believable reasons, it's hard to really have a show. Most series consist almost entirely of regulars interacting and dealing with conflicts. Even on procedural dramas, where the problem is "the case," and not the other characters, they are usually together almost constantly.

On a show set predominantly at a workplace (or other place characters must go to every day), the main source of conflict tends to be that these very different people are forced to be together and deal with one another. The dramatic or comedic focus is on conflict-laden relationships that are battled over there. Similarly, a show about a family tends to focus on conflicts within the family. So, the central premise tends to believably put the characters in one another's constant company for the foreseeable future.

This need for togetherness and interpersonal scenes accounts for the "wacky neighbor," which is a staple of comedy series—where neighbors seem to come over much more frequently than in real life. Or the group of friends who are *always* together and hanging out in a group and never seem to be working their jobs or having separate/ alone time.

Even some shows set at a single workplace can struggle with this issue, because in many workplaces, employees aren't constantly in proximity. Take a department store, for instance. It could be hard to set a show there if the employees' jobs would not put them in one another's presence on a regular basis. (A mall would be even more scattered.) That's why small offices work so well—where people's desks are literally right next to one another. A contained setting tends to lead to the kind of interpersonal conflict scenes that television thrives on, more than a sprawling one, where characters have lots of freedom to be physically separate and little reason to be forced to interact.

Freedom is not something we generally want to give our characters. Hemming them in with challenges makes for more compelling television, in general—even in terms of how they can't escape the other people on the show, much as they might like to at times.

"Believable" Checklist

If your idea can live up to this five-point mission state-ment, it should be "believable" enough:

1. When people read or hear my logline/synopsis, they understand all of it, and have no trouble buying into any of it.

2. It's focused on believable human beings whose attributes, decisions, and actions seem real, given the situation.

3. The backstory and "rules of the world" are clear and simple, easy to grasp, and explained at the very beginning.

4. Everyone's motivations for what they're doing are clear, make sense, and are relatable on a human level.

5. The main entertaining "hook" of my premise, while grabby and intriguing, also feels like it could really happen.

6

LIFE-ALTERING

"What are the stakes?"

This is one of the first questions a professional reader asks about any story idea as they consider it—whether out loud or in their head. What they're really trying to assess is, "Why should an audience care?" Because they know that audiences have a hard time getting emotionally invested in a story unless it's clear that something really big is at risk, which they can easily feel something about. As writers, if we don't have the audience's emotional investment, we don't have anything. They will stop reading and will not feel positive about what they read. We have to hook them into caring, really *caring* about what's going on.

If we have a relatable main character who we're punishing in a believable and original way, we're on the right track, but an audience might still be lukewarm if what the character is trying to achieve doesn't *matter* enough. There has to be a point to all of this—a reason why this journey is worth taking. That means an eventual outcome that is at risk and that represents a tremendous swing between life being great and life being terrible for the main character, and possibly others in the story the audience comes to care about. If that's not clearly there, in the idea, and in the first act of our story, it's hard to get people to willingly devote their time and energy to what we've written.

Sometimes high enough stakes are obvious, like when lives are at risk. But in many story ideas, it's not clear how things will be incredibly, unacceptably worse if the story goal isn't reached—and perhaps far better if it is. I say "perhaps," because the potential negative stakes tend to be the most compelling and important. When there's a lot to lose, there's a lot for the audience to empathize with. (A character who could be killed is in a more compelling situation than a character who could win a lot of money, for instance.) But most successful stories combine positive and negative stakes, meaning that there is a possibility for things to get much worse than they are, but in a happy ending, not only has that been avoided, but things are actually now better than ever.

Stories across all genres are often about massively life-changing situations—once-in-a-lifetime battles where everything is on the line. This is true in terms of both the external stakes—the basic life situations that will be altered, one way or another—and the internal ones, which are how the main character feels about life and themselves, and the attitudes they will take with them, moving forward. In the best stories, life is usually "altered" in both these dimensions.

But the external comes first—especially on-screen, where delving inside the main character's thoughts is harder to do. What's going to initially grab the audience (and the professional reader) is the level of importance of reaching the story goal in their "external" living situation, relationships, and overall prospects for a decent, healthy, happy life—for the main character, and/or others who they heroically fight on behalf of.

Usually what's at stake has something to do with inter-personal relationships and conflicts within them. There's a great gap between what the main character wants from other people and what they're currently getting. They need other people to change how they view and act toward them for life to truly be better. Isn't that how most of our lives are? Most of what we consider problems are really a result of the world of other people not treating us in the exact way we want to be treated, whether it's in terms of money and career, intimate relationships, popularity, etc.

Even in movies where a magical situation creates all the story problems, as in *The Nutty Professor* or *Field of Dreams*, the challenges that ensue almost inevitably play out in the arena of interpersonal relationships.

Internal Stakes Are Not Enough

While it's true that certain novels and stage plays might focus more on a character's internal world as the place where all the conflict and stakes are, in more commercial fiction or theater (and in all works for the screen), it's characters' outer-life situations that have to be primarily at stake. There may well be meaningful internal changes and growth, but what really gets the audience invested (and the industry gatekeepers interested) are the external stakes. That's what our logline, synopsis, and pitch should focus on: "What is the external problem and challenge that needs resolution here?" The internal arc can be implied or briefly mentioned, but first and foremost, one needs to present massive external stakes. Think of which of these you'd rather read and watch, based on the following two loglines:

*A clown fish who is overly protective of his son
must learn to let go and trust him as he sends him
out into the big scary world of growing up in the
ocean.*

*When a clown fish's son is taken by a man on a
fishing boat, the father embarks on an adventure
through the ocean— with few clues—to try to find
him. Meanwhile, the son tries to plot escape from
the dental office aquarium he's found himself
in—which looks like a death sentence.*

Finding Nemo is about both these things—the inner journey of father and son on the subject of the son's independence and the father's letting go—and the outer journey of trying to find and save the son. But it's the outer journey that is exciting and draws people in. The inner journey just gives it depth. When we're pitching an idea, what gives it depth is not primarily what appeals to people. They want to know what makes it an entertaining story challenge in terms of external stakes and actions. And that's true when they're reading the script, as well. Depth is great, but first we need external stakes.

Life-and-Death Stakes

The biggest kind of stakes are obviously "life-and-death." If lives are clearly threatened (or have been taken), then the writer's job becomes easier. No one can say the stakes aren't big enough if people are dying or about to die. Perhaps that's why so many successful stories employ life-and-death stakes. Some writers and filmmakers *only* do projects where life is at stake. Look at Quentin Tarantino. Or any crime novelist or TV cop show creator. Life is at stake in virtually all stories about war, space adventures, major crimes/heists, natural disasters, "one man under siege," superheroes, monsters, and everything in the thriller, horror, and/or action genres.

I would say roughly half of the produced/published stories out there have lives threatened and/or taken as the main problem of the story and the primary thing that the main character is trying to stop, prevent, or get justice for. If we take comedies out of the equation (which virtually never have life-and-death stakes), it would probably be significantly more than half. And there's a good reason for this: it's not easy to hook millions of strangers into really caring about a story. If people they connect with could die, or are trying to save lives or stop a killer, it's easier to get them to care.

The greater number of characters who are actively threatened, the greater the stakes—so if all of humanity could die, then we're pretty much at the top of the mountain, stakes-wise. But even a story about a single individual fighting for their life has exponentially higher stakes than a movie where life isn't at risk. I would caution, though, that "fighting for one's life" stories require the main character to be actively battling against opposing forces in an entertaining way, and with some hope of winning, however small. Fighting diseases or other medical maladies doesn't tend to offer these possibilities—unless the focus is on a heroic doctor, and not the patient. If the main character or a loved one is simply dying, and there's not really much they can do about it, then we've got the opposite of entertaining. We've got "bleak." Audiences don't tend to want to watch "bleak."

In detective stories, someone has already died, usually, so it's often not that someone's life is actively under threat all throughout the story. But there's a killer or killers on the loose, and justice needs to be served, so the stakes are still high. There's a reason why crime thrillers and TV shows are almost never about lesser crimes than murder (or perhaps kidnapping or torture): the stakes just aren't as high. It's hard to get an audience to stay glued to their seats (or turning pages) over the challenges of bringing to justice a burglar or an embezzler or someone who committed a non-deadly assault. In the real world, if any of these things happened to us or our loved ones, of course we would care deeply. But in the world of stories that we watch for entertainment, such lesser crimes—either preventing them or solving them—just aren't big enough to command an audience's investment. And the same is true of other lesser threats to one's physical well-being, such as injuries or illnesses. There is nothing like the potential loss of life to get people's attention—and nothing like someone risking their life and/or fighting against those who would take lives, to get an audience on board with some excitement.

I can't emphasize enough, however, that life can't just be potentially at stake, or only at stake, at the climax. In an action or horror script, for example, there must be action and horror (with life-and-death stakes) all throughout the story. Yes, it should build to its apex in the final act, but if the biggest stakes aren't actively at play until then, we haven't really passed the "stakes test" for our story idea. And as we saw in the Punishing chapter, this is a very common problem with scripts—not having a big enough, "high stakes enough" challenge until very late in the movie. Or having "potential" life stakes, but with nothing actively threatening (or even taking) lives throughout most of the story.

Another problem I sometimes see is a story where most of the stakes are smaller, but life-and-death stakes are introduced at some point, changing the tone and even the genre in a sudden way. This makes everything else that people were concerned about before seem trivial by comparison. Whenever life is at stake, nobody will care about anything else until that is resolved. Nothing else will seem important enough to spend their time and attention on.

Psychologist Abraham Maslow's pyramid of human needs speaks to this. Survival comes first, at the bottom of the pyramid. If survival is threatened, one can't even think about higher needs like love, belonging, and purpose. First, survival has to be handled. It's the same in stories. "Death stakes" are a powerful tool and should be handled carefully. Usually, if they're going to be present, they have to be present throughout, in a genre where that is appropriate, tonally, and where we're not trying to get the audience to primarily care about something else of lower stakes.

Assuming we can avoid those pitfalls, life-and-death stakes allows us to check off "life-altering" as one of the seven key criteria for the story idea. What could be more life-altering than losing life altogether? Nothing.

Everything Else

What if we're not writing in the kind of genre or story situation where actual lives are taken or threatened? Most people who aspire to write aren't. They're writing dramas or comedies, typically, where characters have problems, but potential death isn't really on the table. What then?

We have to make sure that what *is* on the table is still somehow big enough. The good news is that in a comedy or drama, nobody expects life-and-death battles, with heart-pounding action and suspense. But for them to care enough to engage with our story, they need something else that feels almost as big, consistent with our genre.

What could be almost as big as "life-and-death"?

Great story ideas focus on something that threatens to alter lives for the negative in a massive and unrecoverable way. (Or promises to change them for the better in just as significant of a way, if the story goal is reached.)

What's ideal is if it seems like the main character's life (and maybe the lives of others they're trying to help) could essentially be destroyed, even if not literally. So, their chance at happiness, success, and living the life they seem destined to live is all on the line.

Most successful stories usually put one of the following outcomes at risk, in descending order from highest to lowest stakes:

1. **Life itself.**

   As discussed, this can range from the fate of all humanity (*Armageddon*) to a single individual (*Gravity*).

2. **Justice for horrible crimes and prevention of future crimes.**

   This covers investigative stories where someone has been killed (*48 Hrs.*, *Zodiac*, *Chinatown*) or hurt in some other very significant way (*Spotlight*, *Erin Brockovich*). Ideally, it's fun to watch the hero(es) try to get to the bottom of things.

3. **Freedom/individual autonomy.**

   The audience feels that characters are trapped in a terrible situation and roots for their escape/release. This encompasses the most severe dramatic situations (*12 Years a Slave*), lighter, more comedic versions of "bondage" (*Office Space*), and everything in between (*One Flew Over the Cuckoo's Nest*).

4. **Keeping one's family/way of life.**

   This can involve returning to one's home safely, as in *The Wizard of Oz*, *Finding Nemo*, or even *Planes, Trains and Automobiles*. It can also work if something threatens to break up one's cherished life situation (*Gone with the Wind*, *Toy Story*, *Mrs. Doubtfire*). Audiences relate to having all that one holds dear threatened or turned upside down. Isn't this close to losing life itself, emotionally speaking?

5. **Being able to happily move forward with one's ideal life partner.**

   In any story where the main thing the audience is asked to root for is a relationship working out, we've got to put something huge in the way of the relationship, right from the beginning, which doesn't get solved until the very end, if at all. That "thing in the way" has to be external—not just the main character's inner blocks to having a relationship. There has to be a big reason staring them in the face why there's no way this will work—like one of them is a vampire or a mermaid. Or maybe one is already spoken for. Or their families are at war. Or they are rivals, even enemies, in some other way.

As *Save the Cat!* says in describing this kind of story (which it calls "Buddy Love"), the audience has to really see that these two are each other's perfect partners, such that their best chance at happiness will be lost if they don't end up together. The tone can range from serious and dramatic (*Brokeback Mountain*) to extremely light (*Wedding Crashers*).

6. **Winning a much better and deserved professional life and future prospects.**

This is a tricky one, because most stories that are *only* about someone succeeding at a particular job do not feel "high stakes" enough to an audience. Jobs alone often don't feel primal and visceral, because one can always get another job. Even in stories about one trying to have their ideal job, if the only negative stakes are not having it, well, most of us don't have that. They'll live.

To make career stakes work, it has to seem like a character has everything on the line, and their entire future path and happiness will be determined by whether one particular "career" opportunity works out or not. They usually need to come off as both morally better than others in that career who would keep them down and unjustly handicapped in their life situation, in one form or another. Thus, we have certain rare stories that are all about a "career pursuit," such as *The Pursuit of Happyness*, *Working Girl*, and *Jerry Maguire*.

7. **Reaching an important prize that could change one's life and self-definition, which a lot has been sacrificed for.**

This is often seen in "sports movies" like *Rudy*, *Rocky*, or *The Bad News Bears*, where the sports goal is really about something bigger and deeper for the main character and others, where we feel they will be forever changed for the better if they can rise to the occasion (and may be stuck in a really dismal life if they can't). It's not that the sports victory itself matters so much or is so compelling. It's what it represents, and what's on the line for the character (and other team members) beyond the sport. We could put *The 40-Year-Old Virgin* in this same category. Losing his virginity in the right way, with the right person, is something that the main character has to do to be able to move forward into a better life.

8. **A chance at happiness (which life circumstances threaten).**

   This is another one that is easy to abuse or misunderstand. Obviously, all characters and all people want to be happy—and happiness is an internal state, even an internal choice. So, for this to work as story stakes, one generally has to externalize the situation somehow and make it seem, again, like the character's one real chance at a decent and happy life is on the line in the story. Somehow their happiness or chance at it seems to be greatly compromised, and it's reflected in their life circumstances and relationships, in such a way that the audience wants them to fix it—as in *Ordinary People*, *Sideways*, or *Inside Out*. (Note how the latter really goes out of its way to externalize this otherwise internal problem.)

These types of stakes have worked, over and over again, in successful stories. Often stories stumble because they offer only stakes that don't quite make this list and don't feel big enough. Such as:

1. **Any achievement (regardless of how difficult and time-consuming it might be) that isn't hugely**

life-changing for the main character and/or others who will follow.

We need to see how the lives of people we care about will significantly change because of it (and in the pursuit of it)—and be unthinkably better or worse as a result. That's what matters—not just the achievement itself.

2. **A job or career success—unless it's a life-changingly important job that definitely cannot and will not ever be available elsewhere.**

   Job/financial success in and of itself will tend not to move an audience (and might even seem trivial or selfish), if nothing bigger is at stake.

3. **Learning something or changing some inner attitude, belief, or personal quality.**

   Too internal. Can work well, though, when combined with high external stakes.

4. **Military battles within a larger conflict, which don't represent one cohesive "mission" of great emotional importance to the audience.**

   War stories generally work better when they're focused on a specific mission with very clear and important stakes to the audience, or are personal stories about the difficulties and costs of life at war. Ongoing "unit histories" or movies about a series of battles or battles within a war that the audience doesn't have a clear rooting interest in tend to be hard to get an audience excited about.

5. **Generalized happiness or well-being, with no specific and significant external life change.**

   Happiness is always the goal, but audiences seem to need characters battling against hugely difficult external circumstances in pursuit of a measurable goal. The internal state or choice known as happiness is too vague and hard to dramatize to sustain a story on its own.

6. **A single decision or inner growth that needs to happen.**

   Loglines sometimes focus too much on what a character "must decide," "must learn," or "must become." These are all internal. While it's true that a character often must rise up internally in order to confront the external story challenge, in the end, the core of the story idea is that outer challenge. Any internal "musts" need to be preceded by, followed by, or otherwise infused with a challenging external gauntlet of some sort that meets the criteria listed earlier.

7. **An unsympathetic person becoming a better person (or pursuing an unsympathetic goal).**

   As we talked about in the Relatable chapter, audiences generally won't be hooked into caring about and wanting to follow an unsympathetic character in the first act, even if they are going to eventually change.

Characters Dealing with Their Stuff

"Life-altering" also refers to what the main character has to go through in order to resolve whatever challenge is at the heart of the story. Part of the reason we need a big, punishing, external difficulty is that it forces the main character out of their comfort zone and into a situation that will test them, grow them, and perhaps change them in fundamental ways. They will never be the same again for having gone through what they went through in this story.

That's why it's important that whatever they're facing is a unique, even once-in-a-lifetime sort of challenge that they've never faced before and that will require them to do things and access capacities within themselves that they've never had to do or access before. Usually characters are in a foreign world or situation during the long middle section of a story, one in which they are an overmatched underdog trying to figure out how to get through it.

Stories are not about normal life, when characters do their normal things in a normal way. Stories are about extraordinary journeys that characters go on because they feel they have no choice. Something so pressing and impactful is happening or has happened that they have only this one option.

Often a hero is reluctant at first, because none of us really wants to have our life severely altered, where a lot is on the line and the outcome is far from certain (and in fact, it even seems likely we'll fail, in most stories). We also tend to have a certain inertia. We might not be completely fulfilled in our current lives, and might even be rather frustrated, but that doesn't mean we're willing to take some big chance. The main characters of stories are the same. Something has to jolt them, and really rock their world, in order to force them to take a leap into some major challenge. That's what the catalyst does.

But the problem is that they tend to rely on their old ways of doing things, of seeing the world and themselves, in the new world of the story. And this doesn't work. But that won't last forever. The story will force them to change that. In fact, that's the whole point of many stories. They alter the character, both externally and internally, so that at the end, they aren't quite the same as what they were. And usually this is a satisfying alteration, one that made the whole gauntlet worth it. The audience gets to go on that journey with the character, and even be inspired by the (usually) positive change they have witnessed.

In most successful scripts, the main character grows out of whatever was most limiting about themselves and their approach to life at the beginning of the story—but only because the story's external challenges force them to. Characters—just like us—don't willingly question or change their internal dynamics. They only do so when they have no other choice. Even characters who have the most room for growth don't make "growing internally" their primary goal in a story. In fact, they more likely resist any seeming pressure to grow. They try to approach the story problem without changing internally. But this doesn't work. And so, we typically see them fail, to the point where everything seems hopeless, about three-quarters of the way into a story.

Only in the final quarter does the main character have one last chance to battle for the result they want. And this battle typically involves some level of personal change on their part, some growth that is meaningful that they will take with them through the rest of their lives, beyond this story. And that's what makes the story really impact-ful—to character and audience.

Unmet Needs and Wants

I think of a good story as being about the most difficult and important thing its main character ever went through, which changed their life forever. That's generally true of feature films, novels, and plays. In some cases, you could say it's true about a television series as a whole, if you add up all the episodes and seasons. But in TV, it's more useful to think of "story" in terms of the smaller stories that make up individual episodes. And in those, nobody's overall life and happiness is generally on the line in a permanent way. (Unless it's the kind of show where series regulars constantly have their lives at stake.)

That doesn't mean what each character is facing in an episode story isn't incredibly important to them. It is. It really matters, and it's all they can think about ... for the length of that episode. It is also usually representative of something larger that is crucial to their sense of themselves and their lives (or their life continuing in a happy and healthy direction), and they feel they *must* resolve it *now*. It's just that resolving it doesn't massively change their lives, in most series. Instead, it takes their lives back to the normal status quo, where most episodes begin and end—which is a life that isn't quite how they want it to be but isn't in massive crisis at the moment.

The best characters tend to want something they can't have, and in a series, they can never really have it, even though it seems vitally important to them. There is something about each character's life that is fundamentally unsatisfying, and there's a distant fantasy version of their life that they can never quite reach—but they keep trying to, in small and specific ways that become the focus of episodes.

These "unmet wants" typically stem from some fundamental human desire or need that we all share. And they're what keep a show going. Each character spends every episode pursuing and grappling with some variation or microcosm of their unmet want. What makes them compelling is that they are also under siege, in some way, by the world around them, and unable to secure that version of their life that they continually wish they had.

On *Everybody Loves Raymond*, for instance, Ray's fantasy would be to get to watch sports on TV, have as much sex with his wife as he wants, and never have to be in the middle of conflicts or be asked to up his game as a father and husband. His wife Debra's fantasy, though, would be to have a husband who does just that—who understands her, helps her, takes her side, and keeps his annoying parents at bay. Neither of them will ever be able to get their fantasy lives. And that is essentially what the show is about—the conflict between that fantasy and their reality. Virtually every story on that series stems from this.

While it's true that some TV characters also have murders to solve, patients to heal, cases to argue, or zombies to kill, most dramas—and virtually all comedies—use one of these basic unmet fantasies for each important character to drive their stories and to grab the audience emotionally. Most stories are about the characters entertainingly pursuing what they think will make their lives better and/or grappling with what seems to be making their lives worse, around that central fantasy. Ideally, the audience can understand and connect with these fantasies and enjoy watching them play out every week.

Usually this "fantasy" is a character's primary wish for their life, which has something to do with the way others treat them, their place in the world, and their basic life situation. It's usually bigger than any one job, relationship, or measurable goal—although a specific episode might focus on something smaller like that. Usually it connects to love, belonging, respect, freedom, and/or the ability to succeed in one's chosen best life. It's about what life could be like, and what they wish it were like—if they were seen how they want to be seen and got to live the life they most want to live.

In a series idea, I look for that one central thing that each important character is most haunted and challenged by—that one way in which they don't have the life they want, and never will. Because they don't have this, the characters—as in other types of stories—are generally not happy. They may have moments of satisfaction and resolution, but mostly they suffer and struggle. And they are consistently focused on how life is not giving them what they want in some specific area that obsesses and frustrates them. Their "stakes" are all about that.

But unlike characters in a movie, novel, or play, TV characters don't ever resolve or change this, or the show would have to end. The core of any series are these ongoing problems for characters—and ideally, one big problematic situation that affects everyone. Only very limited change is possible, because these difficulties need to remain with them all the way through the series, as its focus—for episode after episode after episode.

"Life-Altering" Checklist

If your idea can live up to this five-point mission state-ment, it should be "life-altering" enough:

1. The stakes of the overall story problems clearly match one of the items in the stakes list in this chapter.

2. The main focus of the characters' problems, goals, and actions are all in their external life situations, not their inner lives.

3. Those stakes are present throughout the story(ies)—not just in the last half or last quarter.

4. The negative consequences of possible failure are clear, growing, and relatable on a primal human level.

5. It's a once-in-a-lifetime challenge for the main character, and it forces them to consider some fundamental changes. (In a series, episode stories are about microcosms of such a challenge, with limited character change.)

7

ENTERTAINING

They call it the entertainment business for a reason.

When writers are paid, and have a career at writing, it's generally because they have figured out how to entertain audiences. Their work does this consistently and substantially, to the point where people will pay for the experience.

Sounds simple, right? However, most writers don't start out making it a priority to be entertaining. They instead focus on a lot of other things, which may be important but generally won't lead to success in the marketplace unless "entertainment" is added in a big way.

Entertainment is tied to genre. Audiences consume particular genres because they expect certain kinds of emotional experiences from them. They want to laugh, be scared, be moved, be fascinated, see amazing action spectacles, be whisked away to a fantasy world, etc. Part of the writer's job is to figure out which sort of "entertainment" they want to provide and then to effectively provide it.

Think from the audience's perspective. What makes anyone pay to consume a story? What motivates them to cough up money for Broadway tickets, or a movie, or an HBO or Netflix subscription? What inspires them to make the effort and commit the time to check out a novel?

It's generally because they want to be entertained. They think the experience of consuming said story will engage them emotionally in positive ways that they enjoy. They decide to put their precious time, money, and attention into something and are looking to get something back. They're a consumer of a product—not so different from any other product they might pay for and hope to get a certain result from.

And so, like purveyors of any other sort of business one hopes to have a large, happy, paying customer base for, writers look to provide the kind of value that audiences seek.

But that's not quite so easy or straightforward to achieve. For one thing, audiences can't tell us exactly what would most entertain them. They don't tend to know they would like something until it's presented to them. They might point to what they have liked in the past. But a writer can't just repeat or copy what they've already consumed and expect the same impact.

Writers generally need to start by making sure our project would entertain us, first, and that we love it. In order to create our best, most authentic and impactful work, regardless of genre, we need to have real passion for it, and it needs to please us. Nobody else will ever love it if we don't love it first. But in the end, we are trying to create certain kinds of emotional experiences in strangers, as well. To manipulate their feelings.

Most writers didn't begin because they wanted to do that, exactly. Many don't even think about trying to be entertaining. Most don't start out in obvious entertainment genres, but instead write dramas that don't have action, intense suspense, comedy, or other obvious entertainment elements to them. Instead, they chronicle normal life in a kind of realistic way.

This is good in the sense that believability is a priority. And as we've said, writers who sacrifice the "real" on the altar of entertainment usually find it backfiring. It's just that if one ends there, they often miss the point, in terms of what might make their work sellable—because they haven't truly endeavored to entertain, and haven't given the audience enough reason to want to pay for and stay with their work.

Helping the Audience Escape

To be entertained is to escape one's normal life, in some way. We get to experience elevated emotions, of one sort or another, which are fun to experience—while engaging on a deep and committed level with someone else's life experience for a period of time. Successful stories generally find some way to take the audience out of "normal real life" and catapult them to a realm where it's really enjoyable to be.

It's almost like candy—a favorite movie, TV show, book, or play. One *delights* in it. It's a joy to consume, even a guilty pleasure. It's amazing the way one can feel so good, and so outside one's everyday existence, while engaging with the story. Normal life and time seems to stop, even, and one is almost sad when it's over or when they have to stop watching or put the book down. We've all felt that way before, and maybe it's part of why we wanted to be writers—to create stories that have that powerful of a positive impact on people.

This means going beyond simply writing something that interests us. Being interesting is good, even necessary, but it's not enough. The previous paragraph didn't describe what people do with a story that's merely interesting. It described a powerful emotional engagement.

No matter how much is "interesting" in our stories, that's only a tiny fraction of what makes people consume them. They're looking for stories to grab them emotionally and to take them into a feeling state of some kind, in addition to being interesting. In fact, if it entertains them enough, it doesn't necessarily even have to be "interesting" at all.

Being hugely entertaining is the trump card that can commercially outmuscle all of the other six PROBLEM elements. If you are massively entertaining to enough people, you often get a bit of a pass on things like originality and meaningfulness. You may be able to stretch believability a bit more than most, if you're careful. And the audience may not have to relate as deeply to specific characters if what is happening is so riveting to watch or read that they're constantly hooked. Probably the only other element that has to be there, in all its fullness, is "punishing." Because it's very hard to be wildly entertaining if you're not putting consistent pressure on your character(s). The two seem to go hand in hand.

But I wouldn't take this as a license to not take the other five elements as seriously, or to assume one's work is *so* entertaining that it will rise above the pack. The best and most successful stories—including the kind that will get an unknown writer noticed—usually have all seven.

Feelings We Like to Feel

To entertain someone means to go beyond just telling audiences a story that they find relatable and compelling—even one where they can feel for the characters. That is all essential and good, but it doesn't tend to be enough to make a writer successful.

Instead, the process of watching (or reading) the story should be a pleasurable one, in and of itself, where its people, actions, activities, visuals, sound, etc., are consistently enjoyable to focus on.

And it's not just that it's pleasurable. It has to bring them to fairly intense emotional states consistent with the genre. The audience is actually hoping to experience these when they consume a story. In other words, if it's a comedy, they're going to be upset if they hardly ever laugh. If it's a thriller, they better feel fear and tension throughout. Every genre has its emotional "hit" that the audience is looking for.

But not every type of powerful feeling is desirable and sought after in entertainment. For instance, no one pays or tunes in to experience despair or guilt. And it's usually not "entertaining" to watch characters deal with money problems or medical challenges or bickering relationships or many of the other things common in real life. We consume stories to escape from all that and to be stimulated into feeling one or more of the following "entertainment" emotions, which can be mixed and matched and can overlap with one another:

1. **Amusement**

   We all like to laugh, and comedies of various kinds are mainstays in any medium. But when people take in a comedy, they're generally not looking to be mildly amused every once in a while. They're looking to laugh, preferably out loud, as much as possible. It's kind of the whole point. It's what got them in the door. If a writer isn't going to really work to make that happen, but is going for more mild or occasional comedy, then they might want to make sure they're also strongly stimulating one or more of the following emotions, to compensate.

   It's easy to fall into the trap a lot of writers fall into, where they don't fully embrace the task of trying to make people laugh because that sounds too broad and silly to them. So they call their work "dramedy," and say it will have some humor but also be kind of a drama. This can work at times, but often such scripts aren't really that amusing and also lack the kind of truly dramatic situations, spectacle and stakes that could compensate for the lack of real comedy.

2. **Fear**

Like roller coasters or haunted houses on Halloween, stories can be a safe place to experience terror and panic. Somehow seeing someone else go through it, where we share the emotion but aren't at risk like they are, is a fundamentally attractive thing for lots of people, especially when there is some resolution in the end—when the source of the fear has been vanquished, and someone the audience relates to survives.

3. **Fascination**

It's not easy to make people become truly fascinated with what they're seeing play out in a story. It usually requires presenting them with something that has real emotion to it, real stakes, and real spectacle, where they can't look away. Something about it is so intriguing that they are eager to observe it, get more of it, and get to the bottom of it. When things are larger-than-life, are outside their experience, and seem like they really matter, audiences become fascinated. But take note: something can be *interesting* but not *fascinating*. Fascination is more active, emotional, pointed, and extreme.

4. **Shock/outrage**

Story twists and turns that really throw us—that shock us—get our attention. So do wild and unpredictable characters and events. Entertaining stories tend to explore outrageous situations and characters who are far outside our normal experience. It can be fun to watch and react to these people and things, as long as they are believable and there is something relatable at the heart of the story.

5. **Lust/carnal desires**

There's a reason we like watching beautiful people looking and behaving in ways that stimulate desire on some level. If a movie tried to entertain with only pure lust, it would probably be considered pornography, but honestly consider how much audiences enjoy watching certain performers in certain roles, because this is a factor. And it's not just a matter of casting. It's a matter of writing characters and situations in such a way that you can imagine the audience accessing these basic emotions on some level as they watch people do what they do.

And it doesn't just apply to people. It can apply to material objects, cars, homes, lifestyles, even landscapes. Whenever an audience is thinking, "Damn, I wish I had that," or, "That is some serious eye candy," you are activating this emotion.

Take a look at movie trailers and note how consistently they play on these sorts of feelings, be it through actions/explosions, sex, or just amazing visuals that are meant to wow us with their awesome spectacle. Some trailers play on all three of these, and literally every shot in the trailer is going for a kind of visceral "lust response."

6. **Excitement**

Similar to fear, where our hearts are pounding with concern about what might happen next, excitement is when we feel like we're being swept along on an amazing ride of some kind, and we're breathlessly engaged with what is happening. It feels like it's taking us away into a situation where everything matters, and what's happening thrills us—not unlike a great sporting event, where every moment has our attention and we're completely invested.

In writing, tension is something we always want to cultivate. This way, the audience is caught up in the emotion and conflict to a really high degree, and everything that happens just turns the screws further in a way that's really gripping to watch. They're on the edge of their seats or turning the pages as fast as they can. They've lost all sense of time and space and are totally engaged.

7. **Awe**

This is a cousin to lust/carnal desires. Awe goes beyond mere eye candy. We can be awed by the scale of something we're seeing, the difficulty of a challenge, or qualities of a character. While lust might make us go, "Damn," awe will make us go "Whoa." It's more of an openmouthed, wide-eyed wonder, like walking into Willy Wonka's main chocolate room for the first time, or watching Jake LaMotta fight Sugar Ray Robinson in *Raging Bull*. It's not necessarily a positive thing. It's just . . . awesome.

8. **Romantic love**

   In stories focused on romantic relationships, we
   tend to become one of the characters, emotionally.
   We relate to what they're going through. Romances
   elicit strong emotions of connection with another
   person, of being seen, understood, supported, and
   wanted—of bonding with someone we really want
   to bond with. In romantic stories, we generally have
   to strongly identify with the main character's desire
   for their chosen partner. Of course, something has
   to get in the way of that desire for there to be
   conflict, but living vicariously through the
   emotions of love is a highly attractive and appealing
   experience for most people.

9. **Empathy/compassion**

   We should always relate to the main character of a
   story in some way, but if we take "relatable" to an
   extreme, the audience might feel such incredible
   bonding with a character that they start to love
   them on a deep level and feel everything they feel
   intensely. It's almost a love affair between audience
   and character. This sense of human connection can
   be really pleasurable.

10. **Eager anticipation**

Stories that work create anticipation for the audience: a desire to see what's coming next, to keep turning the pages, to keep watching, no matter what. This usually means big and important conflicts are at play, with huge stakes, and the audience can't wait to see how they play out. It also means the plotting creates surprise and unexpected twists, even shocking or outrageous developments.

At the end of the day, we want our audience to care so much about our characters and what's going on that nothing else matters for them while they're in our story. They are completely swept away. They have become the characters, and what's happening to them really matters. So much is on the line, and so many high-conflict factors are in play, and so much is changing because of fresh actions by our main character and the forces against them, causing so much mayhem, and so much intrigue, that the audience is kind of rubbing their hands together, thinking, "I can't wait to see where *this* leads," and, "How is she possibly going to deal with *that*?"

Ingredients to Add to "Drama"

If our genre is simply "drama" of one sort or another, without life-and-death stakes, we might have an uphill battle, because drama, on its surface, doesn't have an obvious method for entertaining audiences. It can feel flat, boring, and "real-life" (meaning not escapist at all). Or it can even be bleak and depressing. One has to work extra hard to find those elements within a drama that will really grab the audience and become their "candy." Dramas tend to be hard to sell if they don't have some other genre interwoven with them and/or aren't based on something that was previously very successful in another medium.

For a "straight drama" to be entertaining to a large audience, without life-and-death stakes or some procedural investigation element, it usually needs to feature certain additional entertainment elements. The following is a list of ten that are commonly used. Note how each of the thirty film and television examples show up in at least two categories each—meaning they add at least two of these elements to their "drama."

Comedy

- *Glee*
- *Jane the Virgin*

- *Gilmore Girls*
- *Six Feet Under*

- *Forrest Gump*
- *American Beauty*

Rich, beautiful, possibly famous people

- *The O.C.*
- *Downton Abbey*
- *Nashville*
- *Beverly Hills 90210*
- *Dallas*
- *Dynasty*
- *This Is Us*
- *Empire*

- *The King's Speech*
- *Sunset Boulevard*
- *The Social Network*
- *Amadeus*
- *Citizen Kane*

High-spectacle period settings

- *Downton Abbey*

- *Gone with the Wind*

- *The King's Speech*
- *Amadeus*

Major betrayals, backstabbing, hidden agendas

- *Empire*
- *Jane the Virgin*
- *Dallas*
- *Dynasty*
- *The O.C.*

- *Amadeus*
- *Casablanca*
- *The Social Network*

Music as an integral element

- *Glee*
- *Nashville*
- *Empire*

- *Amadeus*

Entertaining-to-watch activities with lots of spectacle, conflict, emotion

- *Friday Night Lights*
- *The Sopranos*
- *Six Feet Under*

- *Schindler's List*
- *Amadeus*
- *Gone with the Wind*
- *Raging Bull*

Major amounts of sex, romance, and conflicts/rivalries over same

- *The O.C.*
- *Friday Night Lights*
- *Jane the Virgin*
- *Downton Abbey*
- *Gilmore Girls*
- *Beverly Hills 90210*

- *American Beauty*
- *Gone with the Wind*
- *Casablanca*

Outrageous people

- *The Sopranos*
- *Empire*
- *Jane the Virgin*
- *Dallas*
- *Dynasty*

- *Forrest Gump*

- *American Beauty*
- *One Flew Over the Cuckoo's Nest*
- *Good Will Hunting*
- *Citizen Kane*
- *A Beautiful Mind*
- *Amadeus*
- *Rain Man*
- *The Social Network*
- *Sunset Boulevard*
- *Raging Bull*

Intriguing foreign worlds

- *The Sopranos*
- *Downton Abbey*

- *Schindler's List*
- *The Shawshank Redemption*
- *One Flew Over the Cuckoo's Nest*
- *Amadeus*
- *Gone with the Wind*

Inspiring depictions of love/family shining through, despite major conflicts

- *This Is Us*
- *Gilmore Girls*

- *Downton Abbey*

- *Forrest Gump*
- *A Beautiful Mind*
- *Good Will Hunting*
- *The Shawshank Redemption*
- *Rain Man*

You might notice a common theme here. All these elements tend to make things "larger-than-life" for the audience. The stories exaggerate real life in some way that makes them really fun to watch.

Rich, Sexy, and Glamorous

On one-hour television, these extra elements to augment "drama" can be especially important. When we don't have life-and-death stakes and procedural "cases" (or the constant comedy that half-hour shows tend to have), we

...mething else that makes audiences really want to
... Some combination of these elements tends to be
...essary for commercial success. And the more the better,
...ally. Successful shows tend to have many of these things
working at once.

Television is as much about providing an escape from normal life for its viewers as movies, novels, or plays are. Perhaps more so. We tune in at 9:00 p.m. on a Sunday because we want to be swept away into something that really engages and entertains us. Generally speaking, we're not looking to watch normal life, with all its mundanities. We want to see characters on some sort of "adventure of the week," where certain problems have arisen that they must deal with—and when they try to, things spin further out of control.

Comedies have an easier time of it, in some ways, because if they're truly funny, almost anything goes. One can depict a very wide variety of characters and situations on television, and if it makes people laugh, it provides the escapist entertainment they're looking for. Comedies don't need to depict exaggerated life situations as much, and can be more about the "everyday," as long as they deliver laughs.

Dramas don't have it quite so easy. They have to find some other way to provide that escape. And if it's not life-

and-death stakes, it usually means providing some wish fulfillment for the audience in the form of characters with lives most of us don't have but might fantasize about. For this reason, drama series are often filled with really attractive and wealthy people with lots of story conflicts related to their romance and sex with other attractive and wealthy people. That's typically not the entire show (or it would be straight soap opera), but it's an important element of many prime-time dramas. The audience is fascinated to live vicariously through the characters—not because their lives are similar to their own, but because they live in a larger-than-life world.

Ideally, the characters are still relatable, and even complex and deep, and the writing incisive and real. But this "sexy soap" element is still a key part of the appeal for many drama series. Fame, power, money, beauty, glamour, sex, and high spectacle of some kind are typically in the mix and are all a part of what provides "candy" for the audience.

Many one-hour pitches I've heard (and some I've pitched myself) that don't quite work are earnest portraits of real life, with all its somewhat sad compromises, without anything to really excite the audience and transport them to somewhere that is fun for them to be.

One-hour concepts that sell generally focus more on the escapist element. Ideally, they're also "about something" more than that, and present believable, memorable characters who the audience connects with. But writers tend to stumble when they don't realize they have to take care of the "entertainment" challenge, first and foremost, with any series idea.

"Entertaining" Checklist

If your idea can live up to this five-point mission state-ment, it should have a good chance at being entertaining enough:

1. I'm clear on what sort of emotional entertainment experience I'm offering my audience—and why it's desirable to them.

2. Fans of this sort of story (or series) and this genre will get what they pay for—because I make that central to my mission here.

3. Something larger-than-life makes my story/series feel like escapist "candy" to its audience—so they're always wanting more.

4. It focuses on elements with a primal, universal, emotional hook for the audience—it's designed to make them *feel*.

5. I will keep surprising, intriguing, and delighting them with how my story/series plays out and what my characters do and say.

8

MEANINGFUL

S ay we've got a fresh and original story idea that has
solid entertainment value built into it through a
specific genre, with a relatable main character who is grow-
ingly punished as they actively pursue a goal with truly life-
altering stakes, in a way that all feels completely believable,
understandable, and real.

If that is the case, we're way ahead of most writers. And
if professional readers agree that we achieved all of those
things (which, of course, is a big "if"), then we might truly
be off and running with the project. But there's one other
thing they—and audiences—might ask. One other thing
that can be the difference between the project really going
somewhere and not. And that question is . . .

the point?

...ning, why did we write it, and what is the audience ...sed to come away with in the end? What does it ...plore that goes beyond its specific plot, characters, and scenes that has some relevancy and value in their own life—or the human condition in general—that they can take with them, so that it's not just a brief and forgettable ride?

In other words, what is truly meaningful about it at the end of the day—to the characters and also to the audience?

What Is It REALLY About?

What we're talking about is theme. Theme refers to the universally relatable questions about how to best live life, and solve the problems in it, which underlie many stories. *The Godfather* might be about the son of a mafia don who takes over the family business to protect it, but on a thematic level, it's about loyalty vs. individuality, family vs. country, and innocence vs. experience. It explores these issues, which don't have easy answers to them, in a rich way. And it makes the film much more than just an exciting gangster movie. (Though it is also, quite pointedly, that.)

Meaningfulness is probably the most optional of the seven PROBLEM elements, in the sense that projects can sometimes succeed without it. If a story is entertain. enough, especially, audiences can partially forgive it fo being totally lightweight and forgettable.

But for starting a career and being seen as a formidable writer—and for creating powerfully impactful stories—meaning matters greatly. The greatest, meatiest, and most memorable stories say something, somehow, about deeper concepts that resonate with people in a significant way. These are the kinds of stories that become truly beloved by a culture, that win awards, and that make a writer's name.

Theme emerges by examining competing priorities in life through the specifics of a story, which ultimately reflects a point of view about the best way to be in the world, and the most effective way—at least in a situation like the one at hand. I'm not talking about facile, obvious arguments, like whether racism is good or bad or whether one should be selfish or giving. A good theme weighs competing goods or competing evils against each other, and dramatizes why it's so difficult to make a choice some-times, or to change. It doesn't offer easy answers. Any thematic outcome or judgment in the end is earned, grad-ually, over the course of the story. It's not just thrown out there in a quick and easy way.

Theme often occurs to a writer—and starts to be explored—fairly late in the writing process. It doesn't have to be there from the beginning. In fact, it can be better that it isn't. Some writers start with theme—what they feel they want to say—and make that more important than telling a solid story, one that has all the other six elements. This usually doesn't work so well. Such themes will tend to come off heavy-handed and overly simplistic, and the writer can be handcuffed by their theme obsession, such that they are unable or unwilling to really fulfill the other six elements.

Whether ideas for theme are there from the outset or not, they will tend to grow and flower later in the process, after the other elements of story have been worked out. It might even take multiple drafts before the key themes really make themselves evident. But at a certain point, theme deserves conscious attention, to make sure that the underlying questions of a story are being effectively explored and developed.

This may be the trickiest part of writing because theme is not right there on the surface. It's a subtle, underlying set of dynamics that colors everything but never quite takes the foreground. The audience's focus is always on character, dialogue, action, and plot. Within and behind all that is theme, but it can be hard to put your finger on.

I'm intrigued by the "Dramatica" theory about how stories work. Its basic premise is that the most complete stories have four different "throughlines" going on at once. The first is the personal story for the main character. The second is the overall situation that all the characters are concerned with. And then it adds something really interesting: the idea of an "influence character," whose presence stimulates the main character to consider changing in some fundamental way. The fourth throughline is the relationship between these two characters, which is generally the most passionate, important, and in-depth relationship in the story.

This "influence character" is usually not the antagonist. Often, they're an ally, love interest, or mentor—like Hannibal Lecter or Obi-Wan Kenobi. Or Julie in *Tootsie*. Or Furious in *Boyz n the Hood*.

Just making sure a story has such a character and relationship can add a depth and personal element that it might otherwise lack. It's a similar concept to what *Save the Cat!* calls the "B Story"—which is usually a relationship that has some major conflict to it, and which carries the theme. That theme is often tied up in the main character's arc and to what extent they change at the end. This relationship is what tends to push that potential change.

Dramatica suggests that each of the four throughlines also explores a particular thematic conflict between two opposing values, which consistently crop up in its scenes. So, while one throughline might explore confidence vs. worry, another might focus on instinct vs. conditioning.

Whether or not we buy into Dramatica's take on it, this is the most elusive aspect of any story—how to subtly communicate these themes beneath the surface of our characters and plot in a way that seems believable and natural but still resonates in the end.

It's also tricky to believably track character change. It has to feel earned. A very common note on scripts is that someone seems to change suddenly and arbitrarily in the end, and we didn't see the progress and causes of that change in a believable way. They seem to just instantly be different in the end because the writer wants them to have changed. But it hasn't been layered in successfully throughout the script, such that readers feel the realness of that evolution and buy into it.

Somehow theme and character arc have to keep coming up, and developing throughout the story, for the end result to make sense and land with the audience. Whatever pressures make the main character even consider changing

e idea. But
final piece
weight and

ers to these
It was just
sidered that
some stories
writers want
ven why they
where is that
sonal connec-

y our own life
eliefs, so that
ay. Ideally, the
to us, beneath
plot. Our fasci-
reating. And it
ue judgments of

ry
enter
into a sy
we would
s so that the re
really "about." Bu
the story will definiti
es and character change
could all seem too pat.
hese within the arcs of
he script itself, readers
without being overtly

hat a story is about,
for: "What are you
e it, why could only
his, and what's the
k this because the
they're trying to
g from. But they
ed by the other

go further, to

atic questions are
about. If we led with
them, or sell them on th
e deal of their interest as the
e whole project feel like it has

metimes a writer won't have solid answ
estions and hasn't really thought about it.
an interesting idea to them—they hadn't con
it had to have a larger "point." And again,
don't, and can still be successful. But usually
their work to have meaningfulness, and it's e
wanted to write it, in the first place. So
found? Often, it comes from their own per
tion to the story, and what it explores.

It helps to be inspired, on some level, b
experience or strongly held feelings and I
what we're writing reflects us in some w
story idea delves into something personal
the fictional elements on the surface of the
nations and passions fuel what we're c
becomes an opportunity for us to make val
some kind that reflect our beliefs.

This is not just about making ...
ously "good" and others "bad." C...
judgments tend to not feel real, convincin...
It's more about subtly shading what the audie...
to take away from the various choices, behav...
outcomes throughout the story. We show what wor...
doesn't work, and what the consequences are of the pa...
characters take. And in the end, that all adds up to something. The audience may not be able to put it into words,
exactly, but they feel they have witnessed something that
resonates as meaty, deep, and having a point of view
behind it.

When a script really feels rich and meaningful, the
human condition has been explored in some fresh and
specific way. The journey that the main character takes,
and how they impact their world (and how their world
impacts them) resonates with audiences and has a lasting
effect on them.

Think about how some of the following Academy
Award Best Picture winners and nominees clearly have
deeper themes that one can sink their teeth into. We might
not be able to instantly sum them up in words (though it
might be a good exercise to try), but we can definitely say
they're "about" something more than their surface plots:

Oz

Sunshine

ck Mountain

Aviator

Beautiful Mind

- *E.T. the Extra-Terrestrial*
- *American Beauty*
- *L.A. Confidential*
- *To Kill a Mockingbird*
- *Unforgiven*

These are not inconsequential stories. A lot is going on beyond the surface plot and entertainment. Deeper issues are being examined. And one comes away feeling that meaningful questions in their own life, for society, and/or for life in general have been explored.

Sticking to the Audience's Ribs

There are a number of ways stories can be meaningful and give the audience something to remember and value beyond the fleeting experience of consuming them:

1. They tell us something about—or give us a new perspective on—the world or a specific issue or subculture.

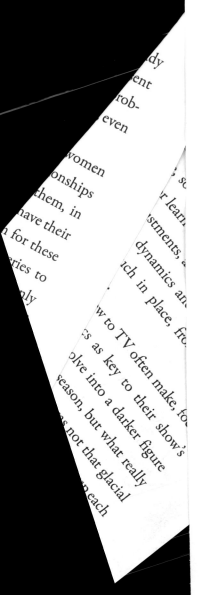

2. They inspire us in our own lives through the character battles, triumphs, and change they depict.

3. They move us, through the good that we see coming through characters as they connect with one another—and as we connect with them.

4. They create a call to action, motivating us to move or act in some way.

5. They make us understand and admire what others might have gone through or are going through.

6. They make us look at how we (or others we know) are like certain characters, allowing us to develop personal insight.

7. They show us how others live, which can provide guidance and perspective in our own lives.

8. They give us a broader sense of the world, its problems, and humanity as a whole.

9. They inspire us toward some sort of change, as a result of what we witness characters doing or facing.

10. They give us hope or emotional sustenance, and help us see that we're not alone.

TV Characters Live

Television can go much

lives and relationships—

can find more "meaning" in

more impactful and satisfying for

characters over a long time period, che

regularly. They become more like real-life

Because of this, a big part of the TV writer's cha

to create a world of people and situations that a large au

ence would want to do that with—where they could easily

get close to the characters and want to stay with them for

the long term.

At the same time, television can't provide the kind of

"meaning" that movies, novels, or plays do, in the sense

that the latter are all about character and life transfor-

mations that are significant and come about because of

a single compressed story journey. Series by their

have to be consistently making an impact, such that the audience will ultimately buy the character's arc.

Theme is not necessarily evident in a logline—which should focus on the main story problem and what's original, punishing, relatable, and entertaining about it. But if we were to expand our logline into a synopsis of a couple paragraphs, up to a full page, we would definitely want to hint at the thematic elements so that the reader of the synopsis gets what the story is really "about." But even then, to come out and state that the story will definitively explore or touch on certain themes and character change tends to make readers skeptical. It could all seem too pat. So, one tends to hide or embed these within the arcs of the story and characters. Just as in the script itself, readers should usually feel and sense themes, without being overtly told what they are.

Sometimes when people ask us what a story is about, theme is what they're really looking for: "What are you trying to say with it, why did you write it, why could only you write it, what is the point of all this, and what's the larger takeaway?" They might only ask this because the idea isn't really working for them, and they're trying to politely understand where we're coming from. But they might ask it because they are intrigued by the other

PROBLEM elements and want to go further, to kind of complete the picture.

It makes sense that thematic questions are the final thing they want to know about. If we led with theme, we probably wouldn't grab them, or sell them on the idea. But it can help seal the deal of their interest as the final piece that makes the whole project feel like it has weight and depth.

Sometimes a writer won't have solid answers to these questions and hasn't really thought about it. It was just an interesting idea to them—they hadn't considered that it had to have a larger "point." And again, some stories don't, and can still be successful. But usually writers want their work to have meaningfulness, and it's even why they wanted to write it, in the first place. So where is that found? Often, it comes from their own personal connection to the story, and what it explores.

It helps to be inspired, on some level, by our own life experience or strongly held feelings and beliefs, so that what we're writing reflects us in some way. Ideally, the story idea delves into something personal to us, beneath the fictional elements on the surface of the plot. Our fascinations and passions fuel what we're creating. And it becomes an opportunity for us to make value judgments of some kind that reflect our beliefs.

This is not just about making some characters obviously "good" and others "bad." Overt and obvious judgments tend to not feel real, convincing, or interesting. It's more about subtly shading what the audience is meant to take away from the various choices, behaviors, and outcomes throughout the story. We show what works and doesn't work, and what the consequences are of the paths characters take. And in the end, that all adds up to something. The audience may not be able to put it into words, exactly, but they feel they have witnessed something that resonates as meaty, deep, and having a point of view behind it.

When a script really feels rich and meaningful, the human condition has been explored in some fresh and specific way. The journey that the main character takes, and how they impact their world (and how their world impacts them) resonates with audiences and has a lasting effect on them.

Think about how some of the following Academy Award Best Picture winners and nominees clearly have deeper themes that one can sink their teeth into. We might not be able to instantly sum them up in words (though it might be a good exercise to try), but we can definitely say they're "about" something more than their surface plots:

- *The Wizard of Oz*
- *Little Miss Sunshine*
- *Brokeback Mountain*
- *The Aviator*
- *A Beautiful Mind*
- *E.T. the Extra-Terrestrial*
- *American Beauty*
- *L.A. Confidential*
- *To Kill a Mockingbird*
- *Unforgiven*

These are not inconsequential stories. A lot is going on beyond the surface plot and entertainment. Deeper issues are being examined. And one comes away feeling that meaningful questions in their own life, for society, and/or for life in general have been explored.

Sticking to the Audience's Ribs

There are a number of ways stories can be meaningful and give the audience something to remember and value beyond the fleeting experience of consuming them:

1. They tell us something about—or give us a new perspective on—the world or a specific issue or subculture.

2. They inspire us in our own lives through the character battles, triumphs, and change they depict.

3. They move us, through the good that we see coming through characters as they connect with one another—and as we connect with them.

4. They create a call to action, motivating us to move or act in some way.

5. They make us understand and admire what others might have gone through or are going through.

6. They make us look at how we (or others we know) are like certain characters, allowing us to develop personal insight.

7. They show us how others live, which can provide guidance and perspective in our own lives.

8. They give us a broader sense of the world, its problems, and humanity as a whole.

9. They inspire us toward some sort of change, as a result of what we witness characters doing or facing.

10. They give us hope or emotional sustenance, and help us see that we're not alone.

TV Characters Don't Really Change

Television can go much deeper into characters—and their lives and relationships—than a single long-form story, and can find more "meaning" in the process. It can also be more impactful and satisfying for an audience to follow characters over a long time period, checking in with them regularly. They become more like real-life relationships. Because of this, a big part of the TV writer's challenge is to create a world of people and situations that a large audience would want to do that with—where they could easily get close to the characters and want to stay with them for the long term.

At the same time, television can't provide the kind of "meaning" that movies, novels, or plays do, in the sense that the latter are all about character and life transformations that are significant and come about because of a single compressed story journey. Series by their nature have to come up with new stories every week that are based on virtually the same kinds of problems and conflicts as every other episode, so it can seem like characters don't really grow, change, or learn much. They may learn a few things, make some adjustments, and evolve in small ways, but their primary inner dynamics and outer difficulties have to remain pretty much in place, from episode to episode and season to season.

This is a mistake writers new to TV often make, focusing on long-term character arcs as key to their show's concept. Walter White might evolve into a darker figure by the end of *Breaking Bad*'s final season, but what really made the show go from week to week was not that glacial evolution so much as the huge problems that came up each episode—all of which were connected to the central problematic situation of the show, which was established in the pilot. Surface changes to the lives of TV characters may come and go, but the main engine of the series in terms of conflicts and challenges (and what the characters are all about) can't.

That doesn't mean the situation they find themselves in, as a series launches in a pilot, shouldn't still be "life-altering." Characters are still faced with some enormous set of challenges, with significant and relatable life stakes. It's just that they can't really resolve them anytime soon—and the episodes of a series aren't about "steady progress toward solving them." Instead, episodes present an infinite number of smaller variations of the larger problem that they connect to, and do resolve in some way, even if the bigger issues don't.

On *Sex and the City*, for example, we have four women battling various challenges in the world of relationships with men—as the main "problem" for each of them, in every episode, for season after season. They each have their own internal qualities that are part of the reason for these challenges, which have to stay in place for the series to keep going. If all this is ever to be resolved, it can only be in the last episode of the last season, where each of them finally has a satisfying long-term relationship situation that seems like it's working, with no more pressing problems—and there's a sense that each has finally grown internally, as well. (Until the first movie, when they need to shake things up again to create more story.)

"Meaningful" Checklist

If your idea can live up to this five-point mission statement, it should be meaningful enough:

1. My story/series explores universal and important human issues, beyond its surface plot, which don't have easy, facile answers.

2. My characters are driven by primal, unmet wants and needs around which there is the possibility for growth and change.

3. The end point of the story/series illustrates some transformation that makes the journey seem worthwhile.

4. There are specific ways in which my story/series is meant to positively impact and affect audiences in their lives.

5. I'm not overtly focused on theme and character arc—they are subtle but meaningful by-products of compelling storytelling.

9
PUTTING "PROBLEM" TO WORK

All of this is a tall order, I know: trying to come up with ideas that meet all of these criteria. But this is why it is so challenging for writers to break through and succeed—and so rewarding for those who do. It's not that the "industry" is too closed off. It's not about "who you know." Or "what's selling." It's not even about dialogue and description, primarily, or story structure. Yes, all those things play a role. But at the heart of it all, for a writer, it's always about a story premise that is "worth writing"—even more than it is about the writing itself. And even writers who are really good with scene writing, dialogue, and story structure struggle with generating winning ideas.

Yet it's the most important part.

Where Ideas Come From

The question of how to "find" great ideas (and whether my ideas were even in the ballpark) has long been daunting to me. Maybe that's why I wrote this book. Over time, I've realized that most of the ideas that I (or others) think "should be a movie" or "could be a series" actually lack some of these key elements, and it's often not easy to reshape them so that they can succeed.

This is just something one has to get past. It happens to most writers. Very few of us create project after project that really "work." In fact, many of the very best movies, series, novels, and plays were one of only a very small handful of projects by their author that broke through in this way. (Sometimes the only one.) Nobody just pumps out winning idea after winning idea and turns them into successful project after successful project. Or at least, almost no one. Most of us have a very low batting average. But we keep going, because something drives us to.

When we talk about idea generation, and where ideas come from, there's also something mysterious to the process that seems to be a bit outside of our conscious control. We can't just take these PROBLEM elements and somehow "figure out" an idea, from nothing, that meets all of them. It's more that we apply these standards to ideas that do come through, in order to evaluate and shape them. But first, we need something to apply them to.

Most of the process of writing is actually about coming up with the next idea—even if it's just for what should happen in the next scene. There's always the need for ideas at every point in the process. And in my experience, ideas tend to come when I find some way to get out of the analytical mode. This usually involves letting go of being stressed about the situation and getting more playful and curious—asking questions and listening for answers. They might show up when I'm taking a long drive or walking or in the shower. Ironically, a large part of the "job" is to relax into allowing the flow of ideas.

Another way to activate this creative mode is brainstorming on some need I'm trying to fill or problem I'm trying to solve. I pose a question—a small and definite question that, if answered, would take me a step forward in whatever I'm writing. If I identify the right question and get out of the way (meaning, relax and trust), answers do tend to come. If I have to, I'll just start listing possible answers off the top of my head—not stopping to critique any of them—until I have ten or twenty. Usually something intriguing will come at some point—as long as I haven't stopped and become critical and analytical along the way.

Finding Story Ideas

What if I don't have any idea of what I want to write but know I want to write something? Then I make it my job to start noticing what I'm interested in. As I consume others' work, live my life, and observe, I notice stories I really like and would like to emulate, and also what I'd like to explore more in life. What am I uniquely and passionately obsessed about? What bothers me? Excites me? Moves me? I keep track of these things.

I actually have a document on my computer with several columns full of random fragments that have crossed my mind that I might want to write about. One column is full of people—occupations, life situations, types of potential characters. Another column contains topics that are part of life on planet Earth. A third column is for arenas or worlds of activity. Another is for locations and settings.

These can be very mundane on their own, but you never know where a story idea might come from. One practice is to look for the most extreme, outrageous, or difficult version of something that we otherwise think of as everyday. (Like a bachelor weekend in Las Vegas—which led to *The Hangover*.) Or the most unexpected, entertaining, or brand-new version of something. Because that's the kind of thing that a viable story tends to be based on—not the everyday version, but the hugely, provocatively exaggerated one.

Another helpful practice is to brainstorm on combining seemingly disparate elements to see what that produces. When I'm in the mode of looking for what I want to write next, I might set aside fifteen minutes a day and decide to generate five ideas during that time. Maybe that sounds impossible to achieve, but with the right tools, it isn't. I take an item from one column, pair it with an item from another column, and see if anything comes.

I'll go down those other columns, one item at a time, looking at how I might combine my first item with any of these other items and what that might lead to: "If I had to write a story that combined aliens with baseball, what might it be?" Then, "What about aliens and genetic medicine?" "Aliens and hippie environmentalists?" My list might have a hundred things on it that I'm trying to mix "aliens" with. Nothing might come to mind for most of those. But you'd be surprised at the intriguing story possibilities that will pop into my head about some of them—just a sentence or two of a possible concept to explore later.

Then, on another day, I could be starting with baseball and looking to combine baseball and genetic medicine, then baseball and hippie environmentalists, etc. Eventually, every item in every column can be considered with every other item to see what might emerge.

I don't spend a lot of time on this—again, it's light brainstorming. I just look for a few seconds at each possible pairing and see what might spring forth as a basic story situation I can jot down in a rough logline. And then I'll move on and keep going until I've done that day's "homework."

If I do this for a single month, even just on the weekdays, I'll have one hundred ideas. Then I look them over. I might not want to further pursue a single one of them. But I might. And I may see common threads that generate new ideas.

The basic principles that seem to work for me are:

1. Note things that you like and are interested in, in the world and in other stories. Keep track of these.

2. Focus on generating lots of ideas.

3. Schedule a (short) regular daily time devoted to this.

4. Create a brainstorming tool of some kind that stimulates mental connections between different potential story and character elements.

5. Don't edit, critique, or try to figure it all out. Just lightly consider possibilities and jot them down.

6. Know your preferred genres—study them and make them part of the process. (While being open to stretching into new ones.)

7. Sit with potential story fragments or questions and expect answers to come at odd times. Focus on being relaxed and playful about it.

8. Spend regular time chilling out doing activities during which ideas tend to come—things like walking, driving, biking.

9. Last, but not least, work to understand what makes a viable story idea—its key elements—so that it becomes second nature to you as a filter you apply to every potential idea.

Again, the goal is lots of ideas and an ongoing process for generating, recording, and playing with them. Your new mission, after all, is not to jump into writing the first thing that intrigues you. Because now you realize the job of a writer is a lot less about writing than you thought—and much more about deciding what to write: "the idea."

Talent Is Overrated

Because writing is such a competitive field, where there are a very limited number of paid jobs or sales, compared to the vast numbers of people who want to be doing it for a living—and a system designed to keep most of them out until they can demonstrate the salability of their work—it's easy to get caught up in thinking of it in terms of "haves" and "have-nots": that there are the elite who are talented and thus successful, and then there's . . . everybody else.

I like what Akiva Goldsman said about this at a rally during the 2007–08 writers' strike. He was then one of the most successful screenwriters in the business. (He won the Oscar for *A Beautiful Mind*.) Throughout his life, he said, people kept telling him to "stop"—that he didn't have what it took to make it as a writer. The secret of his success? He just never stopped.

There's much wisdom to that simple statement. I don't know that any of us are born talented. Things might come quicker or more innately for some than for others, but most of our early scripts (and early drafts of our current scripts, even) are not "good" in the sense that others would read them and want to get behind them. In my view, "talent" (i.e., that thing some people have that allows them to succeed) is almost entirely about attitude and practice, and not native ability.

For all of us, on every project, there is a continuum of growth from writing something that nobody thinks shows talent (i.e., it doesn't grab the audience as believable, compelling, and fresh the way successful writing needs to) to writing something that others say does show talent—and proves you have it.

On my first professional writing gig—a script for an episode of *From the Earth to the Moon*—I wrote many drafts that my supervisors, to be frank, didn't think showed much talent, if any. (But apparently I must have had some, based on other things I had written that got me the job.) They continued to give me notes, and I continued to work to address them.

Eventually, I turned in a draft that, to me, was less than 10 percent different from the previous draft (and I'd lost count of the number of drafts at that point). But to others, it pushed the script over the edge into something that was good. And suddenly their perception of my talent for this project increased greatly. Suddenly my script worked, and I was asked to rewrite some of the other scripts. Did something change within me that made me suddenly have something I didn't before? No.

The difference between the perception and experience of "I don't have talent" to "I do have talent" is not about innate worthiness or ability to do this, but about attitude and actions along the way as one strives to do better and better at what all of us writers are here to do—which is to communicate with others and engage their emotions.

Anyone can do that, in their own unique way, if they really choose to and stick with it. So my advice is to stop wondering if you "have it" or not. Take that out of the equation. You have it. What makes you one of the special ones who succeed is what you do with it.

About the Author

E rik Bork won two Emmys and two Golden Globe Awards for his work on the HBO miniseries *Band of Brothers* and *From the Earth to the Moon*, writing multiple episodes of each and working on the creative producing team—for executive producer Tom Hanks (and Steven Spielberg on *Band of Brothers*).

He has sold original pitches and written television pilots for NBC and Fox, worked on the writing staff of two primetime drama series, and written screenplays on assignment for Universal Pictures, HBO, TNT, and Playtone. He's worked as a writer for such production companies as Imagine Entertainment, Original Film, director Doug Liman, Warren Littlefield, Jerry Bruckheimer Television, NBC Studios, ABC Studios, Warner Bros., Sony Pictures, and 20th Century Fox.

Erik has taught for UCLA Extension's Writers' Program and National University's MFA in Professional Screenwriting program. He has been called one of the "Top Ten Most Influential Screenwriting Bloggers," and offers one-on-one coaching at www.FlyingWrestler.com.

The Idea is now an online course! Learn a systematic process to apply the principles in this book with video lessons, new content and examples, a 100+ page workbook and optional monthly coaching sessions. And get a free mini-course on great loglines, all at:

erikbork.thinkific.com

Printed in the USA
CPSIA information can be obtained
at www.ICGtesting.com
LVHW021532290823
756642LV00001B/39